ATHEISM AND LIBERATION

ATHEISM
AND LIBERATION

Antonio Pérez-Esclarín

Translated by John Drury

ORBIS BOOKS
Maryknoll, New York 10545

First published as *Ateísmo y liberación,* copyright © 1974 Editorial Fuentes S.R.L., Caracas, Venezuela

English translation copyright © 1978 by Orbis Books, Maryknoll, NY 10545

All rights reserved

Printed in the United States of America

Library of Congress Cataloging in Publication Data

Pérez Esclarín, Antonio.
  Atheism and liberation.

  Translation of Ateísmo y liberación.
  Includes bibliographical references.
  1. Christianity and atheism.   2. Liberation
theology.   I. Title.
BR128.A8P4713   261.8   78-731

ISBN 0-88344-020-2

CONTENTS

v

INTRODUCTION

I have never been able to comprehend how Christianity, which is essentially a message of liberation, managed to allow the rise of the capitalistic system and then came to safeguard it. This fact is all the more lamentable and incomprehensible because injustice, oppression, and manipulation are the most striking and obvious features of that system.

The reign of idolatry is now firmly implanted in Christian civilization. The law of the golden calf now prevails in the name of God. People today—even those who say they believe in God—have given over their hearts to their things and possessions. It is these that define humanity and worth. Fellow human beings are merely rungs on the ladder toward the possession of more and more things. Trodden down and turned into an anonymous mass, the vast majority of human beings look up to the top of the pyramid where a small minority enjoy the benefits of luxury, waste, and arbitrary whimsy. The law of might makes right continues to determine relationships between nations, peoples, and human groups, though it is disguised under developmentalist statistics, myths about aid, and innocuous smiles.

In this dehumanized world we find a pallid Christianity living the life of a vegetable. All the revolutionary and creative import of its message of love seems to have been lost. The Christian faith seems to have been stripped of its subversive content—i.e., its commitment to the creation of an ever more humane world and its opposition to every type of dehumanization. It now seems to entail nothing more than a theoretical acceptance of certain vague principles or the practice of certain cultural and social acts. Until very recently the label "revolutionary" was practically synonymous with the label

1

"atheist," for the simple reason that Christianity had become radically debased. But in truth it is the label "Christian" that is most nearly synonymous with the true meaning of "revolutionary."

This book is framed in terms of a dialogue with humanistic atheism. In the name of both God and human beings it joins atheists in rejecting an idolatrous and inhuman world. It is an affirmation of atheism vis-à-vis all the false gods that dehumanize people and help to maintain bondage and injustice. If a religion does not begin by undermining the bases of an unjust system, then it cannot claim any connection with the biblical concept of religion. For, as the prophets and Jesus made clear, the Bible sees religion as the concrete practice of justice. Authentic acceptance of God means accepting a God who impels people to construct a more humane and fraternal world and to eradicate every trace of oppression. If one worships a God who does not do that, then one is worshipping a false god, an idol. For the true God has revealed himself as our liberator. He has made it clear that faith in him must be translated into the concrete practice of service to others and love for other people.

Thus this work is also meant to be a profession of faith in the true God. This God revealed himself in an act of socio-political liberation. From creation on, he has invited us to participate in the fashioning of real communion. In Jesus Christ he becomes the very embodiment of liberation and guarantees definitive victory to all human beings, both atheists and believers, who are committed to constructing his utopian kingdom here and now on earth.

PART I

THE IDOLATROUS CIVILIZATION

1

ART, ALIENATION, AND PROTEST: HUMANKIND TODAY IN THE VIEW OF THE ARTS

The political life of a people is but a superficial aspect of its existence. If we want to become familiar with its innermost life—the wellspring of its activity—we must penetrate its very soul through its literature, its philosophy, and its art. For they reflect the ideas, passions, and dreams of a people.
—Romain Rolland

Ezra Pound noted that artists are the "antennae of the race." They lay hold of the vague feelings and personal experiences floating around them and project them for all to see. In *Art as Experience* John Dewey compared them to the lofty peaks in a mountain chain which heighten and give life to the monotonous rise and fall of the ordinary ridges.

Art is the expression of a people, a culture, a way of life at a given moment. It is a confrontation with existence and a response to it, crystallizing a particular moment in the life of the whole. To know the art of a people is to penetrate their feelings and scrutinize their heart. Hence it is possible to explore the history of humanity's aspirations and values by examining the

5

history of its art. From the dolmens and monoliths of the paleolithic age to the frenetic art of our own day, humankind has left us a record of its most authentic desires and values.

Art was born in the bosom of religion. Primitive art was vitalistic, sensual, organic, and fraught with religious symbolism. It boldly sought to transcend humanity's earthly experiences of a reality that seemed quite hostile. The paintings on the walls of prehistoric cave-dwellings show us human beings struggling for life and vying with the supra-terrestrial forces that control it. One can readily detect a sense of the sacred and the numinous in the carefully arranged monoliths that make up the awesome megalithic structures of a primitive age.

In their art the Egyptians sing of divinity and humanity, of the life hereafter and the transforming power of human intelligence. The sides of their pyramids mount steeply toward the apex, toward union with heaven and the deity. The processional aisles of their temples draw our attention toward the transcendental meaning of that which lies beyond our present life. Yet, at the same time, it is human intelligence that shines through the serious, pensive faces of their hieratic figures.

Greek statuary and architecture reveal a people wholly committed to the art of living. It was a period of human splendor, a golden age of beauty and optimism. Humanity was idealized and rendered perfect as the gods were stripped of their transcendence. The marble sculptures of Phidias captured moments of glory, optimism, and triumph and turned them into eternity. It was an age when people fought with their gods and knew how to die with a challenge on their lips, as Homer and the great dramatists reveal to us.

Rome was pragmatic and glorious. The conquering city was lavish with its bridges and highways, its aqueducts and theaters, its arches of triumph and its monuments to victory. Roman art followed its legions. Extremely realistic, it gave historic embodiment to the triumphalist dreams that stirred its people. Equestrian statues and hieratic busts of the great Roman patricians populated the world that Rome had conquered. And the poems of Virgil resounded through the captured provinces as so many echoes of a glorious chant.

The Middle Ages were a period when people's lives were filled with their faith and their religion. Their culture preached detachment and elevation, and supernatural yearnings filled their hearts. The soul of medieval people can be found in Dante's *Divine Comedy*. Medieval people admired reason (Virgil), but it is only divine revelation (Beatrice) that opens the gateway to heaven. The Gothic cathedrals, straining toward heaven, embody the profound faith of medieval people. They are poems of faith converted into stone. The floorwork, statuary, and stained-glass windows seem to mount toward the stone needles pointing to heaven, trying to detach the viewers from earth and concentrate their thoughts on what lies beyond and above. And when the theater does come into being, its archivolts of sainted figures are matched by its themes, which are primarily concerned with the mysteries of faith.

The Renaissance was pagan but glorious. It marked a return to this earth and this world. Petrarch initiates it in literature with his quest for simple elegance and his love-torn sonnets. In painting Giotto is the first to create a three-dimensional world that breaks with the verticalism of mosaics and stained-glass windows and imbues the faces of his figures with sentiment and emotion. In Renaissance art humanity seems to be full of life and caught up in a frenzy of glory. *Homo* is the center of creation, sung about in romantic tales and sonnets and embellished in the Apollinean busts of Michelangelo and the radiant Venuses of Boticelli. Like the figures of Donatello, human beings are now full of energy and vitality. Their horizons are infinite, as infinite as the newly discovered lands. If Dante may be regarded as the prototype of medieval man, then Leonardo da Vinci is the prototype of Renaissance man: thirsting indefatigably for knowledge and beauty, and combining delicacy with depth and enigmatic overtones.

Baroque art was one of antithesis and paradox. It was the art of the Counter Reformation, which was caught up in the tension between reason and faith. People's minds were quickened by the triumphant advances of the sciences, but their hearts still submitted to the dictates of their faith. Baroque art is the art of a soul that is tense and dislocated. We can see the tension in Don Quixote, in the heroes of Calderón and Shakespeare, in the elongated figures of El Greco, and in the chiaroscuro of Rembrandt, Velásquez, and Ribera. Descartes is baroque, holding back publication of his treatise on metaphysics because Galileo had been forced to retract by the church. So is Tasso, who feels he is unable to write a Christian epic and insists on being examined by the Inquisition, who keeps revising his splendid *Gerusalemme liberata* (1575) until he turns it into the pious *Gerusalemme conquistata* (1595).

The sensualism and bourgeois twists of the rococo period led to a brief revival of classical ideals of purity and clarity. But this in turn soon gave way to the explosive cry of Romanticism as the human spirit sought to expand and to escape the sluggish weight of the Baroque period. Romantic art was a cry of liberation, a return to nature, and a re-enkindled love for the Middle Ages. Pirates, adventurers, saints, and knights on horseback were glorified and sung about because they lived amid tension and risk. Fresh appreciation was lavished on subjective, emotional love, the sensitivity of the senses, the miraculous and even the satanic arts. Intuitive, dreamy individualists, the Romantics experienced their orgy of freedom in the outburst of 1789. It is freedom that vibrates in the determined faces of Goya's dead, in Delacroix's vigorous brushstrokes, and in the sonorous strains of Beethoven's symphonies.

And what about modern art? What does it have to tell us? What image of humanity and human values can we glean from the artistic products of the modern age? In his *Voices of Silence* André Malraux suggests that the imprint of the Roman Empire was engraved on the head of a Roman patrician, and that the medieval saint displayed the humility, renunciation of the world, and yearning for heaven that marked the Middle Ages. What, then, do we find reflected in the naked, splintered human figures of modern painting and sculpture and in the anonymous heroes or anti-heroes who struggle with life in modern literature?

We do not have to be experts to see that anxiety, the search for self, and protest are the clearest and most profound traits embodied in modern art. When we cast our eye on the human beings depicted in modern art, we find broken, famished creatures who are crushed under the weight of their solitude and are yearning for light. They are anxiety-ridden beings who are desperately searching for their lost personal identity and the ability to engage in communication. They want to escape from their anonymity, but they are buffeted by an oppressive, mechanized world that has transformed them into anonymous ciphers in the herd.

In the early part of this century Kafka depicted the puzzlement and emptiness of people today in his prose writings. In the late forties, the age of anxiety served as a theme for the poet W. H. Auden, the French writer Camus, and the American composer Leonard Bernstein. Today those features seem endemic to our art and literature. In them we see and hear the fissured soul of contemporary humanity, the cries of fear and pessimism, the search for light and peace. God is almost completely absent from modern art, but God's death has not given rise to any gloriously self-confident human being. We find no triumphant echoes of Nietzsche's Overman or of Marx's utopian paradise. Modern art speaks of a dead God and a dying human being. It speaks in the accents of Rabbi Rubinstein, who felt obliged to adopt atheism in the face of the Nazi atrocities and God's silence: "When I say we live in the time of the death of God, I mean that the thread uniting God and humanity, heaven and earth, has been broken. We stand in a cold, silent, unfeeling cosmos, unaided by any purposeful power beyond our own resources. After Auschwitz, what else can a Jew say about God?"[1]

With no God and no faith in earthly or terrestrial paradises, modern art rejects messianism in general. It is a protest that for the most part does not presume to offer any solutions. Many artistic works seem to aim to do nothing more than evoke the presence of disorders, oppression, chaos, and the absurd; to depict a "sound and a fury signifying nothing." They simply point to the sore and protest against it.

In my opinion, this protest is the greatest merit of modern art. Indeed we might say that modern art is protest: against the massification and depersonalization in affluent cultures, against the structures of oppression that keep people down in underdeveloped nations. Wassily Kandinsky has stressed the relationship between a work of art and its age, and we do well to remember it: "Every work of art is the child of its time; often it is the mother of our emotions. It follows that each period of culture produces an art of its own, which cannot be repeated. . . . Only just now awakening after years of materialism, our soul is infected with the despair born of unbelief, of lack of purpose and aim."[2]

Here, then, I propose to view contemporary humanity through the eyes of our artists. We shall try to glean the features of humankind's face and soul from our painting and sculpture. We shall follow its trembling steps in the novel and the cinema. Perhaps that will help us to become better acquainted with our modern world, so weary of itself and straining anxiously toward the future, so devoid of God, faith, and a soul of its own.

My ambition here is modest, however. I am not naive enough to think that I can offer a full and complete picture of modern art in these pages. I do not propose to do that, nor do I think that is necessary. I shall simply allude to some characteristic artists and works of art in order to evoke the soul of contemporary humanity that lies buried in their efforts. Perhaps we can piece our soul together from the fragments buried in their lines and verses, thus detecting the way to greater meaningfulness and authenticity. For, as William Barrett points out, "art is the collective dream of a period, a dream in which, if we have eyes to see, we can trace the physiognomy of the time clearly."[3]

Literature

Perhaps no one has gotten closer to the pulse of contemporary literature than Thomas Wolfe, that great poet of solitude and loneliness. At least his words may usher us into our examination of the modern theater, modern poetry, and the modern novel: "Naked and alone we came into exile. In her dark womb we did not know our mother's face: from the prison of her flesh have we come into the unspeakable and incommunicable prison of this earth."[4]

The theater. It is the theater, even more than poetry or the novel, that presents us with the most depressing picture of contemporary humanity. Perhaps this was inevitable, as Roy McMullen suggests. Since the theater explores everything and serves as a bridge between illusion and reality, it could not help but be fascinated by the modern problem of authenticity.[5]

In any case the fact is clear enough. Since Ibsen's day the major playwrights have been at one in stressing the feelings of meaninglessness and absurdity. Classical tragedy remains dead since the days of Racine, for it is structured around a world of values that are certainly not ours any longer. We can admire an Orestes or a Hamlet, but we fully realize that they belong to some distant past. They are vestiges of some bygone history whose beliefs and values are not ours. The same holds true for the theater of honor for which Lope de Vega and Calderón de la Barca wrote, even as it does for the philosophico-religious theater of Tirso de Molina. The motivational structure and fabric of that day is gone for good. Honor, dignity, sincere and self-denying love strike us as outmoded and quixotic. Our reality today is a much more abject one.

The modern theater presents us with a human being who is superficial, alienated, broken, and in search of lost identity. This certainly holds true for the works of its major writers: e.g., Miller, Brecht, Ionesco, Genet, Beckett, Pinter, Albee, Adamov, Simpson, Grass, and Arrabal. The human being is depicted as an intruder in the world from outside, a "splinter in the flesh" says Jupiter to Orestes in *The Flies* (Sartre). Roy McMullen notes how symptomatic it is that so many modern dramas should be concerned with prostitution, the very incarnation of inauthenticity: Genet's *The Balcony;* Brecht's *The Good Woman of Sezuan;* Betti's *The Queen and the Rebels;* and George Bernard Shaw's *Mrs. Warren's Profession.* It is almost as if the modern dramatist wants to show us the prostituted soul, a soul that is false, dedicated to superficial pleasures, devoid of meaning and fulfillment. At the close of *The Balcony* (Genet), as Madame Irma turns out the lights in her bordello, she assures the audience that everything in their own homes is even falser than what they have witnessed at her place.

On the modern stage we find human beings who are alone and understood by no one. They vainly seek for warmth in a world where interpersonal communication is becoming more and more difficult. We live our lives talking into a tape recorder, says Beckett (*Krapp's Last Tape*), because no one is listening to us and no one is interested. We live as strangers, even among the members of our own family. In *The Bald Soprano*, Ionesco depicts a world in which people talk to each other but never really communicate. In one scene a man and a woman happen to meet each other and strike up a conversation. As the conversation proceeds, they discover that they both came from New York on the ten o'clock train and both live in the same building on Fifth Avenue. Even more surprising, they both live in the same apartment and have a seven-year-old daughter. The final surprise is their discovery that they are husband and wife. As Ionesco sees it, words have become falling stones, corpses.

In *The Chairs* (Ionesco), an old man wants to communicate his message to humanity before he dies, for it is the message that gives meaning to his life. He has invited the king, the pope, and various representatives of society to hear the message, which will be delivered by a professional orator rather than himself. Minutes before the orator arrives, the old man and his wife commit suicide by jumping out a window. The orator arrives, offers greetings, and mounts the platform. But all that comes out of his mouth are savage, dissonant, guttural sounds. He is a mute. Here, in this work belonging to the theater of the absurd, the whole tragedy of human communication, language, and life reaches its peak; all that remains is silence.[6]

In *Le malentendu*, Camus shows us two women who kill a seeming stranger; he turns out to be the brother of one and the husband of the other. In *Who's Afraid of Virginia Woolf*, Edward Albee shows us all the stark rawness of a world characterized by falsehood, indifference, and inattention. In *No Exit*, Sartre maintains that the realm of interhuman relations is hell itself.

The problem, however, is not just that we live among strangers or enemies. Our own life and being, our very self, is alien to us. In *The Balcony* (Genet), the theme seems to be that the human person as such does not even exist. All that exists is the mask that we present to the world. What lies under that mask does not matter. All that matters is that the masquerade goes on. The reason for being is to create a living lie, something that will impress and deceive other people.

In *Death of a Salesman*, Arthur Miller presents a society that forces its members to be more concerned about the image other people have of them than about their own authentic life and being. Willy Loman is the true prototype of the businessman, wholly dependent on economic success and wildly looking for popular renown. He lives on the opinions of others, without any personality of his own. Indeed he does not even ask himself who he is. He wants greatness based on material and social success, a greatness devoid of depth, spiritual values, honesty, and ethics. He wants to attain his objectives through technique and cunning rather than through honest effort and struggle. He builds his life on false values, loses all sense of direction and purpose, and then is destroyed by the very system he had made the center of his life. His response to that situation is suicide. With cold calculation he gets in his car and drives off to his death. It is Biff who sums up his life in the closing scene: "He had the wrong dreams. All, all, wrong. . . . He never knew who he was."[7]

Suicide is also the decision of Joe Keller in *All My Sons* because he cannot face up to reality. In *Long Day's Journey into Night*, the Tyrone family commits slow suicide with alcohol and drugs because its members cannot accept a realistic look at their lives.

Other dramas depict love as possessiveness, the domination of another human being, and "cannibalism" (Arrabal). In *Amédée or How to Get Rid of It,* Ionesco portrays a marriage faced with a serious problem. A corpse lies on the marriage bed, growing to enormous size. The couple do not know what to do with it, or how to get rid of it, as it gradually takes over the house and makes it uninhabitable. It is the love that once lived between the couple and is now dead. In *Don Juan or the Love of Geometry,* we learn that "marriage is hell."[8] Many other dramatists—Adamov, Genet, Ionesco, Buzzatti, Arrabal, Mrozek, and Jarry, for example—depict an absurd, disintegrating world in which man is enslaved by his family, society, or love. He is a hopeless human being whose only recourse is to laugh at himself or forget civilization and return to a savagely primitive state. He is alone, perpetually and irrevocably alone.[9]

Perhaps it is Samuel Beckett more than anyone else who has plumbed the depths of modern alienation and meaninglessness. His characters are crazy, dying, sick, immobile. Like corruption itself, they simultaneously repel us and fascinate us. Beckett strips them of all transcendence and meaningfulness until they are reduced to mere voices. That is all that still lives in them.

Identity is some vaporous thing that his characters may have possessed some time in the past. All that remains in *Malone Dies* is a voice discoursing resignedly on a lost identity and a lost meaningfulness. The world has become a foggy blur obscuring the meaningfulness of things. In *Embers,* the shade of Henry's wife tells him: "The time comes when one cannot speak to you any more. The time will come when no one will speak to you at all, not even complete strangers. You will be quite alone with your voice; there will be no other voice but yours." As Leslie Paul describes it: "It is the ultimate aloneness, which makes a discovery of identity impossible; one has no identity, if nothing else is present."[10] Life is reduced to a hopeful waiting, an anxious search for some unknown someone or something that never comes.

In *Waiting for Godot,* we find a metaphysics of emptiness. Nothingness pervades every line from beginning to end. Time rides at anchor, and everything is as vague and undefined as in a dream. The dialogue is natural, brutally realistic, and larded with silence. In the end no one comes. We do not even manage to find out who Godot is. Rebutting all too facile interpretations that see Godot as a symbol for God, Beckett has insisted that is not the case. Confronted with time, we can only wait. As they wait, the two characters in this play fill up the time with conversation. It is automatic, absurd, useless, and ever moving toward the abyss of silence. Hope seems absurd; the tragedy of the two hoboes is that they must go on waiting nevertheless.

But perhaps Beckett is trying to tell us that our attitude must be one of firm hope anyway; that we must not capitulate; that we must share the meager things we have in friendship and camaraderie, as the two characters in his play do. Hopeful waiting itself implies both life and illusion, even though no one comes in the end.

While *Waiting for Godot* may hint vaguely at an attitude as the solution to the problem of people today, the modern theater tends to focus on the problem of anxiety and absurdity without trying to even suggest that there is any sort of solution. Life is absurd; there is nothing to do but live it in all its absurdity. God is dead; or else he is a mere spectator who does not involve himself at all in human issues (Brecht's *The Good Woman of Sezuan*). With him has died all hope, courage, and illusion. We must live stoically, or perhaps die heroically as does Argia, the prostitute, in Ugo Betti's *The Queen and the Rebels*. As she puts it: "I have lived too long all alone to go to bed with a man." When the rebels holding her persist in their suspicion that she is really the queen they are looking for, Argia suddenly decides to take advantage of this opportunity to rise above her sordid, humiliating life. As she goes to her execution, her words negate the naturalism and emptiness that had pervaded the drama: "How pleasant and serene is the calm that hovers over the hills. . . . It truly is a place for kings, and in it we ought to live regally."

Is that "esthetic" faith the only solution? Is there no solution at all, as others suggest? Or must we take a sudden, irrational leap of faith toward an absent God, as many of Eugene O'Neill's dramas seem to suggest? Perhaps such a leap away from the void toward some Presence is the way we can give new value to our shadowy wandering here. That seems to be the central message of Claudel's dramas.

The new experimental theater has struck out on a very different road. It has rejected the dichotomy between actor and spectator and has set out in search of a more positive and creative attitude. Through self-revelation and encounter, it looks for some way of living in communion and solidarity. So we have the audience participation in the "living theater" of Julien Beck and Judith Molina; the new spiritualization in the "open theater" of Joe Chaikin (*The Serpent*) and O'Horgan (*Hair, Tom Paine, Jesus Christ Superstar*); the theater of La Mama (Ellen Steward) and above all the experimental theater of Jerzy Grotowski, the Polish leader of the avant-garde theater.

Grotowski reworks the great dramas of history: Shakespeare's *Hamlet,* Wyspianki's *The Acropolis,* Marlowe's *Doctor Faustus,* Calderón's *The Constant Prince,* and so forth. He endows them with fresh flesh and blood. The traditional heroes are stripped of all heroism and egotism, of all sense of superiority that separates them from the rest of humankind. They become Christ-like figures or secular saints, oppressed and humiliated: pure symbols of modern-day humanity. The audience reacts by stretching its open arms toward them in an attitude of purification, rapprochement, and love.

More recent developments in the modern theater may not explicitly acknowledge God, but it is clear that they are open to the notion of ritualistic purification. In their sincere effort to help fashion a more humane community, they are completely religious. They hint at new ways of experiencing and living our transcendental and human dimension, thus escaping from the alienation that now eats away at us. It is only when we get back to being real human beings that we will be able to accept the true God once again.

Poetry. It has been said that poetry is too meditative an art for our present age. Perhaps that is why it is more an art of minorities than ever before, and why poets seem to be more discredited in the eyes of the masses than ever before. To label someone a poet is to suggest that he or she is some sort of odd, fantastic being—perhaps even demented.

But poets have a special sensitivity that enables them to go to the bottom of things and problems, to scrutinize their very core. In other ages poets hymned the glory of humanity and the world, joining them together within God's loving embrace. They celebrated the triumphant stages of a history that kept moving toward a new and better future. That sort of poetry, which honored God, warriors, conquerors, knowledge, and science, seems to be mute once and for all. Today poetry, like all the arts, spends most of its energy in protest: against the suffering of human beings without food and shelter, against the ridiculous emptiness of human life, and against the reification of humanity by a blind, omnipotent technology. Humanity is but a piece of paper blowing in the wind, suggests T. S. Eliot.[11] Today's poetry is pessimistic rather than triumphalistic, filled with protest rather than with paeans of praise.

In modern poetry, too, humanity is crushed and broken. Without asking for it or desiring it, we have been dragged into an inhospitable world, a "waste land." Chaos, disillusionment, and tedious satiety reign supreme. Instead of a soul within, modern humanity has a thirsty desert. We know only thirst and pain:

> What are the roots that clutch, what branches grow
> Out of this stony rubble? Son of man,
> You cannot say, or guess, for you know only
> A heap of broken images, where the sun beats,
> And the dead tree gives no shelter, the cricket no relief,
> And the dry stone no sound of water.
> (Eliot, *The Waste Land*, I, 19–24)

Heidegger tells us that a concern for others (*Sorge*) is a basic source of personal authenticity and the essential wellspring of human existence.[12] Modern poetry reveals an egotistical, depersonalized world filled with boredom and disgust. The lifestyle of a whole society is summed up in the words of a society lady who is sated with sex and pleasure but devoid of love and enthusiasm:

> "What shall I do now? What shall I do?"
> "I shall rush out as I am, and walk the street
> "With my hair down, so. What shall we do to-morrow?
> "What shall we ever do?" The hot water at ten.
> And if it rains, a closed car at four.

And we shall play a game of chess,
Pressing lidless eyes and waiting for a knock upon the
    door.

(Ibid., II, 131–38)

Nausea, emptiness, loneliness, chaos: These are the themes
that resound through the verses of modern poetry. In symbolic form Alberti depicts the triumph of disorder over harmony in our twentieth-century world:

And on the lifeless blackboards
The angel of numbers
Lifeless, Shrouded,
Over 1 and 2
And 3 and 4.

The verses of A. E. Housman are filled with loneliness,
obsessed with the death of love. In the poems of Robinson
Jeffers we are plunged into a human jungle ruled by despair
and hatred. Cummings seems to be trying to tell us that everything in this world is ridiculous. And the poetry of Gottfried
Benn depicts history as a punctured, broken thing where science has finished off religion and all sense of value, where
human beings without personality or meaningfulness struggle
in a void:

Fragments,
Discharges of soul,
Coagulations of the twentieth century,
Scars, circulatory disorders of creation's twilight.
The historic religions of five centuries demolished,
Science: cracks in the Parthenon;
Planck with his quantum theory
has converged over Kepler, and Kierkegaard has
    withdrawn again,
Crises of expression and attacks of eroticism:
That is man today.
Within a void,

The continuity of personality
is preserved by his suits,
That last ten years if the material is good.

The same *tedium vitae* can be found in much modern poetry, from the *Cantos* of Ezra Pound to the verses of Joyce Carol Oates. It is finely expressed by León Felipe:

> Oh, these sinister days,
> Lord . . . these sinister days
> Where nothing consoles me,
> Nourishes me,
> Lifts me up.
> Nothing, Lord, nothing at all . . .
> Neither You, nor beauty.

This is the mood of intolerable boredom, alienation, and meaninglessness that seems to be particularly typical of the affluent, capitalistic world. The other clear-cut mood of contemporary poetry is one of social protest, and this is most prevalent in the underdeveloped, exploited world. Since poets are persons of ardent spirit, their hearts cannot help but bleed when they see the inequalities existing between human beings today. While some bathe in affluence, the great mass of humankind still lives a life of wretchedness and misery. On the one hand we have explored the depths of the ocean, extracted nature's secrets, and landed on the moon. On the other hand we have forgotten our brothers and sisters by our side, raising the standard of power over the corpses and bent shoulders of millions. Even the church and Christianity have not managed to squeeze out the juice from their message of love. All too often they have settled down in a pleasant, comfortable lifestyle that completely contradicts their truth and their mission.

Modern poets rarely mention God by name; they do not attack God either. Here again God is the great absent one. Blame for the present situation rests on human beings alone. We are alone, and perhaps our only consolation is to dream of the bygone gods.

So Hölderlin suggested:

> To be alone
> When the gods have died, or walked away, or hidden,
> Is really to die as well,
> So alone that in our death we dream them.

God is absent, and blame for the present situation rests on human beings. Modern poetry accuses us of shutting ourselves up in our own egotism and failing to look at our brothers and sisters alongside us. Hence the poets take their stand with the oppressed, raising sharp protest in their verses. As León Felipe put it: "There are no factions in a poem, no oppositions between red and white. There we have only one cause, the cause of humanity. And, right now, the cause of human misery."[13]

Many modern poets have followed Walt Whitman in unleashing a hurricane of protest against a dehumanized world. García Lorca chanted the deeds of gypsies and vagabonds over against the weight of oppressive power. César Vallejo wrote revolutionary poetry. Pablo Neruda wrote heart-rending sonnets about the tragic pain and suffering in the world. In his biblical poems of protest, Ernesto Cardenal takes his stand alongside the downtrodden, protesting an unjust world and its egotistical oppressors. The world is full of blood, and there is so much that one would like to forget. As Pablo Neruda put it:

> Come and see the blood along the streets,
> Come and see
> The blood along the streets.
>
> I swear it!
> I was there, I suffered,
> And I bear witness.
> Here will be written down that blood,
> Here that love will still keep burning,
> And through this wounded mouth of mine
> All those mouths will keep on singing.

Rise up to life with me, brother.
Give me your hand from the dark depths
Of your sorrow spilt all over.
Look at me from the depths of the earth,
Peasant, weaver, shepherd—silenced.

The same cry of protest against the plight of the workers
can be found in the poetry of César Vallejo and Ernesto
Cardenal. Vallejo asks pardon of the workers, our saviors, for
the fact that we have eaten their flesh without realizing it.
And Cardenal recites the prayer of the modern poor in his
Psalms:

Hear my words, O Lord,
Hear my cries.
Hear my protest,
For you are not a God who is friend to dictators,
A partisan of their politics.
You are not influenced by propaganda,
Nor in cahoots with gangsters.
There is no sincerity in their speeches
Or in their statements to the press.
They talk of peace
While they escalate their war production.

They talk of peace at peace conferences
And prepare for war in secret.
Their lying radios blare all night.
Their desks are crammed with criminal plans and
    sinister expedients.
Their mouth speaks like a machine gun,
Their smooth tongues are bayonets. . . .

Punish them, O Lord,
Spoil their plans,
Mix up their memoranda,
Block their programs.

At the hour of the warning siren
You will be with me.
You will be my refuge on the day of the Bomb.
Him who does not believe in their lying commercials
Nor in their advertising campaigns
Nor in their political campaigns
Him you bless
You surround him with your love
As with armored tanks.[14]

The novel. The most characteristic note of the modern novel is said to be its radicalism. Modern novelists are disenchanted with the human condition. They are distressed, uncertain, pessimistic, and as skeptical as the poets about the promises and successes of modern technology. They also are in rebellion against the injustices of our modern world, with its oppression and its futility. It seems almost paradoxical that in the historical age when human power seems most evident, literature should present us with such a disenchanted and pessimistic vision. But that seems to be the testimony of the best and greatest writers, those whom Peguy described as drawing their words out of their guts rather than out of their vest pockets. According to them, we must accept the fact that we are living in a period of chronic illness, loneliness, and inhuman injustice. We have made the world completely intolerable; and of course God is absent from this world.

Dostoyevsky was perhaps the first great modern writer who was obsessed with the loss of values in the western world and the death of God. Indeed both phenomena were tied together in his mind. The withdrawal of God entailed the death of values. The western world became more and more dehumanized as it turned more and more toward atheism. Hence all of Dostoyevsky's novels deal with the problem of God. As his biographer, Henri Troyat put it; "What torments his characters is not infirmity or fear of tomorrow but God." In *The Possessed* Kirillov complains that God has tormented him all his life, and Dostoyevsky himself might well have said the same thing. He lived the raw struggle and risk of faith.

Dostoyevsky's novels are filled with all kinds of atheism. In

Fyodor Pavlovich we find a practical, sensual atheism. He is readily inclined to believe that neither God nor immortality exist so that he can go on indulging himself in this life. Ivan Karamazov represents a more intellectual type of worldly atheism, rejecting any idea that cannot be verified in experience. The existence of God seems to lie beyond the scope of a mind that can only conceive of three dimensions. Raskolnikov, the main character of *Crime and Punishment,* kills a human being to prove to himself that he is really someone, not just another fragment in an anonymous mass. In *The Possessed* Kirillov is the embodiment of atheistic humanism on both the theoretical and practical level. He is a saint without God. "If there is no God, then I am God," he says. The same idea underlies much of Sartre's writing: Being a human being comes down to the desire to be God.

While Dostoyevsky did sense the decline of western values and experience the struggle of faith in a reified world, he also chose faith as the only possible solution to the problem. He clung blindly to Christ and sought to transform his gospel message into the norm of salvation. In a letter to Madame Von Wisine he wrote: "If someone were to tell me that Christ were outside the truth, and if it were proved that the truth lies outside Christ, I would still prefer to stick to Christ rather than to the truth." In his 1871 *Notebooks* he wrote: "The western world has lost Christ. That is the reason, the one and only reason, why it is dying."

Perhaps subsequent major novels have done little more than underline Dostoyevsky's vision of a dying West. In a thousand different ways we are given the impression that humanity is on its way out. The same fact was seen and proclaimed by another great Russian novelist, Tolstoy. He pointed out that modern life had completely alienated individuals from themselves. The emphasis on rationalism and materialism combined with the humdrum routine of a depersonalized way of life to deprive us of our inner life. No longer could man feel any passion for his own personal existence. Only the discovery of our own personal death could restore our authenticity and help us find the authentic meaning of life (see *The Death of Ivan Illyitch*).

Here we have one of the themes that will recur in Heidegger's philosophy. We are "beings bound for death" (*Sein zum Tode*). Only by continually confronting our own death can we truly commit ourselves to carrying out and fulfilling our own personal project in life.

Dostoyevsky and Tolstoy not only presented the human problem openly and in depth but also tried to offer some solution. The present-day novel, like present-day art in general, is much more pessimistic. It depicts the ennui and absurdity of life without offering a solution. Everything comes back to the same starting point, and salvation appears impossible. Isn't that what García Márquez is trying to tell us in *A Hundred Years of Solitude*, his epic of loneliness and abandonment in a Colombian village?[15]

Absurdity and nothingness have become real-life categories, presences, incarnations of life and people. The modern novel seems to echo Shakespeare's line about life ("a tale told by an idiot . . ."), and the latter is alluded to directly in Faulkner's title, *The Sound and the Fury*.[16] In *The Beast in the Jungle* Henry James shows us the living death of John Marcher, a man who suffers the total futility of living. Incapable of giving or receiving love, he approaches death to find out that nothing really happened in his life. In *El gran momento de Mary Tribune* Juan García Hortelano depicts the stagnation and decay of the bourgeois world and way of life. Nothing happens in life, and it really is not worth the trouble.[17]

The view of life as being absurd reached its zenith in the existential novels and stories of recent times. Camus's *The Fall* and *The Stranger* spell out the absurdity of human existence.[18] Roquentin, the main character of Sartre's *La Nausée*, is assailed by violent attacks of loneliness and illness when he discovers the senseless facticity of objects around him.[19] Virgilio Ferreira pursued this line of thought. In *Nítido Nulo* he offers us a brilliant expression of the existential problem facing people today.

The main characters of Kafka's works are reduced to a pure symbol: K. Fear and loneliness invade them as they struggle passionately and fruitlessly to find a place for themselves as individuals in a closed world that is set against them. In *The*

Trial Joseph K spends a whole lifetime fighting, without ever knowing the battle, the enemy, or the cause. There is "no exit" for him, as there is none for Sartre's characters in *No Exit.* Like Mersault in Camus's *The Stranger,* he goes to his death without knowing why—almost content at being freed once and for all from a false and oppressive world.[20]

In *The Castle* K cannot attain the security he needs in order to be able to live. If he could make contact with the Castle and get the information he needed, then his whole life would be changed. But all the roads leading to it are either closed or obscured. The Castle cannot be reached. All of life is a vain search, and we are tragic seekers of a truth that is never found.

James Joyce's *Ulysses* is another pivotal work in modern fiction. It is a huge compendium of power and paltriness, of beauty and ugliness. It moves on a purely horizontal level, and there is no flight upward at all. Life is enclosed within a vast cycle of routine, not open to anything that transcends it. Hemingway, the great American author, looked to sex and strong emotions for an escape from the suffocating sense of meaninglessness. Man lives amid nothingness, and is nothing himself (see *A Place in the Clearing*).

Among modern Italian writers we find the same ideas expressed. Cesare Pavese (*Lavorare Stanca, Il ritorno all'Uomo*) and Elia Vittorini (*Gerofano Rosso*) give expression to the collective alienation that people feel in their personal lives. Their characters are homeless even among their own friends and relatives. Victims of an inhuman process of industrialization, they are wholly cut off from any possibility of communicating with others. Moravia goes further and presents alienation as the normal condition of modern human beings. As Carlos Gurméndez puts it: "The chief character of *La Noia* feels boredom and ennui as a vacuum preventing any communication with other beings. It becomes the permanent state of his soul. A painter, he destroys his works and stands in front of an empty canvas all the time. . . . Alienation has become an immanent part of his being as an individual, . . . but it also reflects . . . a social situation. . . . The painter and his lover come together because they are both empty vacuums; and they

destroy each other in the vain search for self amid nothingness."[21]

Like the modern theater, the present-day novel prefers to
find its main character in abject creatures. The hero is Every-
man trying to endure and tolerate his own life. It is Norman
Mailer's drunken professor in *An American Dream;* Graham
Greene's wayward priest in *The Power and the Glory;* Julio de la
Vega's chance apostle in *Matías, el apóstol suplente;* and the
whole series of anonymous Christs in contemporary literature.[22] In short, the modern novel has no desire to depict
humanity as glorious or triumphant, as a fitting replacement
for the gods who have been dethroned. Instead it is fascinated
by little people, as we see in the works of Juan Bonet[23] and
Salvador Garmendia.

Like modern poetry, the contemporary novel also raises a
cry of protest against massification and the social injustice that
plagues a large part of humanity. We can see this in the works
of Solzhenitsyn (*Gulag Archipelago, Cancer Ward, One Day in the
Life of Ivan Denisovich*), who denounces oppression, lying, and
injustice that poses under the guise of legality. It is in this same
vein that the best efforts of the Latin American novel are to be
found. Indeed we might say that the search for justice has been
one of the basic themes of the Latin American novel from the
beginning. In an older day the naturalistic novel pitted the
civilizing efforts of humanity against the "barbarity"[24] of the
forests, plains, and rivers. Today the Latin American novel
envisions the revolutionary creation of a new language that will
challenge the old, corrupted language that helps to keep us in
bondage.

The Latin American novel is the best echo of the sorrow and
suffering of our people as they seek to escape their present
state of dependence and acquire an identity of their own.
Denunciations of the situation faced by small peasants can be
found in the Indians of Icaza, Alegría, and Rulfo; in the blacks
of Carpentier; in the farmers of Scorza; and in the people of
the tiny Colombian villages who seem to live only in the pages
of García Márquez. Denunciation of urban alienation and
oppression can be seen in the lonely characters of Onetti, the

office workers of Benedetti, the proletarian figures of Revueltas, the false societal values of Vargas Llosa, the pseudo-
revolutionaries of Garmendia, and the characters of Otero
Silva who are both the agents and the victims of violence.

In the Latin American novel the denunciation of oppression
and alienation becomes a cry of protest and a call to revolution.
It does not simply oppose the oppression caused by a world
whose structures are feudal and whose values are false (Vargas
Llosa, Carpentier, Roa Bastos, Rulfo, etc.). Lately it has gone
further and challenged the lexicon of the established order. In
such works as Cortazar's *Hopscotch* and Lezama Lima's *Paradise*
we find the language of "alarm, renewal, disorder, and
humor."[25]

Not surprisingly, this denunciation and protest is also directed against Christianity and the church. In its view the
Christian God is the God of the white conqueror (Carpentier,
Icaza, Vargas Llosa). His church stands on the side of the
exploiters (Revueltas), wholly out of touch with the suffering
of the common people (Onetti, Arguedas).[26] The common
people have been outraged and oppressed. They are the "suffering Christ" who inhabits the Latin American landscape. But
they have not given up. They have made the decision to keep
on fighting doggedly. Often far removed from the church,
they live a practical Christianity of service and comradeship.
Like the peasants in *Redoble por Rancas,* they have begun to
discover and live out the revolutionary character of their
Christian faith.[27]

I do not want to end this brief discussion of the contemporary novel without mentioning another characteristic feature
of the human beings who inhabit its pages. It is their search for
identity and the terrible difficulty of communicating with their
fellows. In *U.S.A.* Dos Passos depicts a startling picture of
atomistic societal life in that country. Human beings move
about as lonely atoms in a huge anthill. Hungering for love,
they are incapable of truly committing themselves to it. James
Farrell and Sinclair Lewis vent their anger on the depersonalized, herd-like life of the anonymous masses in middle-
class America. In *The Tenants* Malamud presents two writers,

one black and one Jewish. Both are victims of segregation and
each stands in need of the other; yet they cannot establish an
authentic relationship of friendship. The hero of Ralph
Ellison's *The Invisible Man* is a black desperately searching for
his identity. The same theme is summed up succinctly by Leslie
Paul in these remarks on Baldwin's *Another Country:*

What drives young Rufus Scott to suicide from the bridge at night is
not only the humiliation of being a Negro . . . but the impossibility of
being human. That impossibility is realized in terms of race hatred,
but transcends it. . . . To achieve communication first, and after that
love between human beings, is an exploration in which men and
women fail more often than they succeed. . . . This is the theme the
long novel celebrates despite all its ecstatic essays into heterosexual or
homosexual encounters. But what stays in mind, and in a sense stops
the book, making all after anticlimax, is the young Rufus hurling
himself from the bridge, in Oedipean rejection of his faith, weeping,
blaspheming as he falls towards the God he does not believe in.[28]

Without God the whole hierarchy of values crumbles for
want of a basis. People find life more intolerable. In a world of
affluence and overpopulation they feel more and more alone.
The artificial virility of someone like Jimmy Porter, the character in Osborne's *Look Back in Anger,* will not suffice to save us
from the vexation of this loneliness. In a vein similar to that of
Nietzsche and his talk about the Superman, Porter says: "Was I
really wrong to believe that there's a kind of burning virility of
mind and spirit that looks for something as powerful as itself?
The heaviest, strongest creatures in this world seem to be the
loneliest. Like the old bear, following his own breath in the
dark forest. There's no warm pack, no herd to comfort him.
That voice that cries out doesn't *have* to be a weakling's, does
it?"[29] As we shall see further on, however, even Nietzsche
could not tolerate the loneliness of a world without God and
ended up calling him back.

Without God humanity seems to have nothing to hold on to.
We wander aimlessly through the world, dancing to the beat of
our own loneliness. In the obscurity of our disoriented quest
we look for something to lay hold of but cannot find it. We
want some Absolute, some ideal, to give order to things, as does

the main character in David Storey's *Radcliffe,* who tries vainly
to find some justification for his crime.

The avant-garde sexual literature of the recent past proposed to liberate people from the repression that had stifled
them previously. But on the whole it seems to reveal and
produce a world of brutalization and wearisome disgust. At
least that is the impression one gets from reading the works of
Henry Miller (*Tropic of Cancer* and *Tropic of Capricorn*) and
other books which deal with the same general area of sex.
When human beings move from sex partner to sex partner,
trying all the possible forms and positions of love-making
without truly loving, they remain entrenched in loneliness and
anxiety.

Can people today find a replacement for the God we have
rejected? Can we find something to give us complete satisfaction, to let us look on life and other human beings with a smile?
Can we find something to justify fighting on? Or will we be
forced to summon God back again, as Nietzsche had to do? In
all his fiction Graham Greene seems to suggest the latter alternative. His alienated characters find salvation only by ap-
proaching God. Greene, it seems, would have us leap from the
ruins of human life into the presence of God. Or, as Camus put
it: "Faced with the Absurd, these people do not exclaim 'Absurd' but 'God.' " God is the only solution for our situation,
according to Greene. Without God life is too burdensome and
monotonous. Heaven is a conclusion we arrive at insofar as we
touch and feel the omnipresence of evil around us and come to
sense the remote idea of some supreme good.[30]

Arthur Koestler seems to have a similar concern. He wants
to find some overall meaning, some key that will open the
world and humanity to real fulfillment. Similarly Evelyn
Waugh (*The End of the Battle*) suggests to us that abnegation and
sacrifice are the means we must use to rediscover our humanity
and meaningfulness. Guy Scrouchback ultimately makes the
heroic decision to marry a woman whom he does not love but
who needs him. Only then does be begin to find salvation, to
move out of the brutal society that turns human lives into
vacuums.

Perhaps our egotistical and disenchanted world should give

more serious thought to the notion that it is better to give than
to receive. Perhaps out of sheer egotistical concern we should
not be so self-centered and selfish.

The Plastic Arts

Painting. The same message we have encountered in literature is being carved out in today's plastic arts. The abstractions
and distortions we find in modern painting and sculpture
bespeak the same absence of value and meaningfulness. Riddled with anxiety, people are seeking desperately for their lost
identity. They have nothing to say about happiness. Their cry
is a social and metaphysical protest against the present state of
affairs.

The world recorded on the murals and canvasses of today's
artists is a world in which people are once again strangers. Far
from being the triumphant figures of Renaissance art or the
vivacious figures of Rubens's art, people in contemporary art
are figures who have lost their transcendence and importance.
The figures are flattened out on the canvas, and there is no
hint of a vertical direction. All the planes are mixed together.
There is no past or future, no near or far, no climax or
culminating point. Everything is of equal importance or value,
be it a chair, a bed, an apple, a pair of old shoes, or a human
being. The artist puts as much intensity and devotion into
painting mere colors as into depicting a human being. The
person is just another object, suffering from pain and loneliness in the solitude of an opaque world. Commenting on an
exhibition at the Museum of Modern Art in New York, Norris
Clarke noted that almost all the artists seemed to present the
human being as naked and suffering. Not knowing who they
are, people find themselves isolated from their fellows and
oppressed by a depersonalizing technology and the obscure
primitive forces that lie within.

In an earlier era futurism did try to capture the beauty of
speed and the triumph of technology. That attitude has
changed, however, and modern art now tends to be critical of
scientific progress. The tragic experience of two world wars,

the suffocating sense of loneliness, and the seeming inability of science to eradicate hunger and misery have contributed to that change in attitude. Instead of liberating us, science seems to have ensnared us in new, more subtle forms of bondage. Consider the dehumanized, robot-like women of Léger ("Three Women") and the machine-like figures of Juan Gris. In one of his best paintings ("The Return of the Prodigal Son") Giorgio de Chirico depicts God as a marble statue and the returning prodigal as a faceless robot.

Going beyond the realism of Courbet, the impressionism of Monet, and the spiritual tension of such post-impressionists as Van Gogh, Gaughin, and Seurat, cubism would become the classicism of modern art.[31] Cézanne began the move away from objective realism that would typify modern art. All the main trends in current art seem to want to escape from all contact with real-life actualities. They are firmly opposed to realism and rationalist optimism: abstractionism (Kandinsky, Mondrian); primitivism (Paul Klee); metaphysical painting (de Chirico); surrealism (Dali, Miró); abstract expressionism (Delauney, Pollock, Newman, Kline, Rothko); Dadaism (Max Ernst), and the *art brut* of Jean Dubuffet.

Challenging a world and a humanity that has lost its self-awareness, modern painters espouse subjectivism as the only norm. That is why modern art is often so difficult to understand. The painters do not want to represent reality. Instead they want to present some symbol of it that will catch its spirit. Our broken world will find its reflection in the vital symbolic message and the subjective vision of the artists themselves. As Roger Rougemont has put it, these works of art are "snares for meditation."

Much of modern art might be described in the terms that John Berger uses for Picasso's "Guernica." Its power lies in the fact that it is a profoundly subjective work. Picasso does not depict the concrete details of the village, the incoming planes, the explosions, the date, and so forth. In the picture there are no enemies to accuse, and no heroes to praise either. Yet the painting itself is a protest, and one can see that even if one knows nothing about the historical event in question. The protest is to be found in what has happened to the bodies in the picture, to the limbs that can be seen in it. Picasso's painting of them is an imaginative recapturing of what really happened to them. We are forced to feel their pain and suffering with our eyes.[32]

Loneliness, suffering, and protest are to be found in the broken faces and blue bodies of Picasso's work; in the flying figures of Dali; in the empty, lifeless frames of Edward Hooper; in the cabaret girls of Toulouse Lautrec; in the prostitutes of Rouault; in George Grosz's "folklore of the urinals"; and in the protesting figures of Guayasamín. Paul Klee presents the ridiculousness of the world in his painting. Edward Munch describes his art as a "cry in nature." Fierce and antiformalist, Bacon fills his canvasses with empty spaces and blind windows, with human beings stripped bare before their own nothingness. His world is one ruled by death and sex; but it is death as carnage and massacre, and sex as mockery and spectacle.[33] The very titles of Giorgio de Chirico's paintings (e.g., *Melancholy, Nostalgia for the Infinite*) suggest his own interest and commitment. Chagall's work embodies a continuing quest for meaning. And the enormous murals of Orozco, who sought to capture the tragic sense of life, give unequalled expression to the relativization that now eats away at our age.

Sculpture. As far as sculpture is concerned, it is significant that the artists have rejected noble materials for their work. In past ages the grandiose achievements and dreams of humanity were molded in marble and bronze. Today's sculptors prefer other materials: steel (David Smith, Theodore Reszak, Antonio Caro, Norton Kricke); glass and concrete (Alicia Peñalba); aluminum, plastic, and paper; and, above all, iron. Steel has all the traits of this century, notes David Smith: power, structure, movement, destruction, and brutality. Without sheen or color, iron helps to express the artist's gloomy concern with life, the quest for authenticity, and feelings of insecurity and lost selfhood.[34]

The attitude of poverty and humility with respect to humanity and its image has been accompanied by a strong desire to revive age-old idols and tribal totems (Moore, Giacometti, Brancusi, Lipschitz, Calder, Max Ernst, Miró, Picasso, etc.).It is as if people were wholly disillusioned with the image of themselves as glorious beings and now wanted to get back to the humbler conceptions of an archaic time.

Loneliness and alienation also find expression in sculpture. There are the mutilated soldiers and perforated nymphs of Henry Moore—figures full of empty spaces; the stylized travelers of Giacometti; the insect-humans of Germaine Richier; the asymmetrical equestrian figures of Marino Marini; the broken silhouettes of the Peusner brothers; and the fallen figures of Trova. Brancusi's whole output can be described as an ardent search for some absolute. And protest against present-day reality can be seen in the works of recent generations of sculptors. Their electronic brains, robots, wheels, and cogs cry out against the reification and brutalization of people by technology and concentration camps.

The Cinema

Born little more than seventy-five years ago, the cinema has become the most popular art form of the twentieth century. It probably reflects and influences the lifestyle and culture of our day more than any other art form. And in the movies we find the same image of humanity and contemporary civilization that we have found in the other arts.

The terrible difficulty that people have in communicating and loving and the anxiety born of a hollow life pervade all the films of Fellini and Bergman. Fellini's films are passionately concerned with individuals who have no place of their own, who are desperately looking for acceptance and purpose. Fellini wants the viewers to look at the screen and discover their own solitude and meaninglessness. He himself explains why he uses such brusque, sometimes almost cruelly sharp, endings: "If you give films a happy ending, then you tempt people to go on living a superficial way. . . . Some time or some place, they will assume something nice is going to happen and one need not do anything to bring it about. By refusing to put a happy ending in the film, one helps to rid them of their false sense of security. Thus they will have to find their own answers."

We find the same reasoning expressed in Bergman's *The Seventh Seal:*

> Jöns: Why do you paint such nonsense?
> Painter: I thought it would serve to remind people that they must die.
> Jöns: Well, it's not going to make them feel any happier.
> Painter: Why should one always make people happy? It might not be a bad idea to scare them a little once in awhile . . .
> Jöns: If you do scare them . . .
> Painter: They'll think.

Fellini and Bergman do not want the viewer to regard the cinema as a wondrous form of escape, as a way of losing oneself in rose-colored illusions and avoiding the reality of one's own life. They want people to think, to grasp the depths of evil (*The Silence, The Eye of the Devil, Wild Strawberries*). They want people to see and touch their ennui and their opacity to love (*La Strada*). The characters in Fellini's movies are sated and bored: with themselves, with others, and with pleasure-seeking (*La Dolce Vita, 8½, The Satyricon*). Yet even in the midst of their tedium, one can sense the tension of a search for something spiritual or transcendent that promises to liberate them. They are attracted to it but frequently it lies beyond their grasp.

Once the viewers grasp the painful reality of evil, Bergman would have them adopt a life of communication and love, and thus soar above evil. Here is what he has to say about three of his movies: "*Through a Glass Darkly, Winter Light,* and *The Silence* stand together. My basic concern in making them was to dramatize the all-importance of communication, of the capacity for feeling. What matters most of all in life is being able to make contact with another human. If you can take the first step toward communication, toward understanding, toward love, then no matter how difficult the future may be—you are saved. This is all that really matters."[35]

Of those three films, *The Silence* may present the most characteristic picture of Bergman's world. God and love are silent amid a nation at war. All communication is broken off. Two sisters live together, completely separated from each other. While Anna copulates animalistically with the mute servant, Esther is dying a slow death right next-door. Yet against this backdrop of abysmal separation and brokenness Bergman would have us go on living. He wants us to embrace life in an attitude of hope and a quest for salvation.

Like Dostoyevsky, Bergman seems to be obsessed with the religious question that is being erased from the present-day world. In his films one can glimpse the tension of the quest for an absent God. He himself has admitted this openly: "To me religious problems are continuously alive. I never cease to concern myself with them; it goes on every hour of every day. . . . I believe in life, in this life, a life after death, all kinds of life. . . . Art lost its basic creative drive the moment it was separated from worship."[36]

Perhaps it is *The Seventh Seal* that best expresses the tension of this search. The tormented soul of the Knight is that of Bergman himself and of all human beings who feel the gnawing doubt raised by death:

> Knight: I want knowledge, not faith, not supposi-
> tions, but knowledge. I want God to stretch out his
> hand toward me, reveal himself and speak to me.
> Death: But he remains silent.
> Knight: I call out to him in the dark but no one
> seems to be there.
> Death: Perhaps no one is there.
> Knight: Then life is an outrageous horror. No one
> can live in the face of death, knowing that all is
> nothingness.
> Death: Most people never reflect about either death
> or the futility of life.
> Knight: But one day they will have to stand at that
> last moment of life and look toward the darkness.

Bergman is well aware of the obscure, taut sternness of faith in our superficial, materialistic, technologized world. He more than anyone else has given shape to the disquieting silence of God, the anguish and seeming meaninglessness of existence, the suffocating potential of eroticism, and the psychological dismemberment of individuals in today's world. Bergman knows that God seems to be totally absent, as if he were dead. He knows the power of evil in the world, its seeming ability to silence God once and for all. In *The Seventh Seal,* the Knight confesses that faith is a torment. It is like loving someone who stays in the shadows, no matter how often or how insistently one calls. And as death approaches, the Knight cries out to God for compassion, since he feels that God *ought* to be somewhere. In *Through a Glass Darkly* Bergman resorts to religious experience and Christian thought as the answer to the existential void of our present-day world.

Antonioni's films are the most patent presentation of such problems as depersonalization, loss of identity, the absence of love in an eroticized world, and the deification of technology (*Red Desert, Eclipse, Blow-Up, La Notte, L'Avventura*). His desolate fields, empty streets, abandoned buildings, and arms that grope to embrace but never find love speak eloquently of the loss of identity and the death of love. In *The Four Hundred Blows* Truffaut masterfully depicts a vain but desperate search for love and friendship. In *Fahrenheit 451* he forecasts the death of all feeling. He presents us with a future society that is controlled and regulated electronically; in it there is no room for reflection or individual feelings. We find the same theme in Kubrick's *2001: A Space Odyssey.* Hal, a sophisticated robot, is a member of the team. His responsibility is to make decisions even if they go against those of the human members of the crew.

Many other artists in the cinema attempt to defend human transcendence against the menace of a brutal, mechanistic, and wholly industrialized milieu: Antonioni, René Clair (*A nous la liberté*), Jacques Tati (*Mon Oncle*), Alain Resnais (*Hiroshima, Mon Amour*), and Godard (*Week-End, Made in U.S.A.*).

The violence of our modern world is a favorite theme of the current cinema. It has found expression in several major films in recent years, which cover violence of all types. There is the violence of the Mafia underworld in Coppola's *The Godfather;* the violence of the drug traffic in Friedkin's *The French Connection;* the political violence of a fascist, militarized society in Costa Gavras's *Z, The Confession,* and *State of Siege;* the violence that reaches and destroys private life in Pekinpah's *Straw Dogs;* the violence of loneliness, nausea, and sex in Bertolucci's *Last Tango in Paris;* the violence of institutions in J. Troell's *The Emigrants* and other films; the violence of violence for its own sake in *A Clockwork Orange*[37]; and the violence that seems to have become so much a part of us that there is no way out of it (Elia Kazan's *The Visitors*).

Kurosawa, the Japanese director, rudely criticizes the hollow, enslaving bureaucracy of our modern world. Alain Turner (*The Salamander*) criticizes depersonalization, bureaucracy, and consumerism as a threat to liberty. Herbert Ross (*Dreams of a Seducer*) presents us with a world that is alien to us and against which we can do nothing. Damiano Damiani (*Confessions of a Commisar*) seems to be saying that we are living in an insane asylum. Claude Goretta (*The Invitation*) depicts the paltry life of the *petite bourgeoisie* clawing to retain a hold on its usual routine. No one has raged more pointedly against the superficiality of hypocritical practices and the hollowness of middle-class morality than the great Spanish director, Buñuel: *Viridiana, Belle de Jour, Tristana, El ángel exterminador, El camino de Santiago, El discreto encanto de la burguesía.* He also takes sides with the oppressed and the downtrodden: *Los olvidados, El perro andaluz, Tierra sin pan.* With Luchino Visconti (*La terra tiembia*), he bitterly denounces exploitation.

As was the case with the modern novel, we find that this dimension of social denunciation finds its best expression in the new cinema of the Third World. That cinema openly denounces the injustice that immerses whole peoples in poverty and misery; it also condemns the tactics of neocolonialism. For under the guise of paternal concern and developmentalism neocolonialism keeps these people in the grip of poverty and oppression. We might mention the works of artists in many different countries: the Brazilians, Glauber Rocha (*Antonio das Mortes, Cabezas Cortadas*) and Roberto Santos (*Augusto Matraga*); the Chileans, Miguel Littin (*El Chacal de Nahueltoro, El Compañero Presidente*), Rafael Sánchez (*El Cuerpo y la Sangre*), Aldo Francia (*Valparaíso, mi amor, Ya no basta con rezar*), Helvio Soto (*Calice Sangriento, Voto más fusil*), and Raul Ruiz (*Tres Tristes Tigres*); the Bolivian, J. Sanjinés (*El Coraje del Pueblo, La Sangre del Cóndor*); the Cuban, J. García Espinosa (*Tercer Mundo, Tercera Guerra Mundial*); the Argentinians, F. Solanas and O. Getino (*La Hora de los Hornos*); and, moving to the world of Africa, Sara Maldoror (*Sambizanga*) and Gilles Pontecorvo (*The Battle of Algiers, Quemada*).

There is no need for a more detailed review of the contemporary cinema. Incomplete as my survey is, the point should be clear enough. In the realm of the cinema people are once again alienated, lonely beings; strangers to themselves and others, and often victims of exploitation. Once again it is a world from which God is absent, despite the efforts of such important directors as Dreyer and Bresson to keep God present.[38]

Conclusion

No more than a brief summation is needed here, for we are clearly coming back to the same basic point again and again. The contemporary vision of humanity and the world in the arts is one in which both are stripped of glory, meaningfulness, and secure rest. The artistic realm reflects and expresses God's absence from the world, but it does not trumpet his death in glorious flourishes. Sincerely concerned about oppressed humanity, it bitterly criticizes all oppression and hypocrisy. It has harsh words for the egotism of the powerful and for the church's lack of valor in failing to find ways to incarnate its message. Modern art is skeptical about the omnipotence of science, raising a cry of protest against massification, the loss of authentic values, and the "cultureless culture" in which we now find ourselves suffocating.

For all these reasons modern art is a pessimistic art, particularly in highly technocratic societies. Human beings are not proud, erect conquerors in its eyes. They are not cut in the image of the dethroned deities, radiant with optimism and glory. Instead we are seen to be overwhelmed with loneliness, enslaved to technology and bureaucracy, devoid of personal identity and a soul of our own, and caught up in an anxious quest for some ray of light, warmth, and life.

In giving form to the present lifestyle and world and rejecting it at the same time, it is clear that modern art wishes to speak out in favor of human freedom and against enslavement. This protest is more concrete and bloodthirsty in the art of the Third World, which puts its hope in a revolutionary change that will bring about a new world of justice and brotherhood.

Talking about himself, Fellini offers us a fine description of the basic attitude that pervades the developed world: "Like many people, I do not have any religion. I navigate in a fragile little boat that is tossed around by the waves. I live with the doubts and tensions of my own obligations. . . . I think there is dignity in that, in continuing to work. . . . That's life, you say, and now what are we going to do? Today we are more naked, defenseless, and alone than ever before in history. We are waiting and hoping for something—perhaps another miracle, perhaps the Martians. Who knows?"

His words are full of skepticism and weariness, of resignation and pessimism. To my mind they reflect a broad range of sentiments in the contemporary world, and they are a fine reflection of the general vision of present-day art.

For the art of the Third World and its sentiments, perhaps we should turn to the thought expressed in *Redoble por Rancas:* "The fence is not the work of God, little ones. It is the work of the Americans. It is not enough to pray; one must fight." Or perhaps to the thought expressed by José Dolores in *Quemada:* "Authentic liberty cannot be given to one as a gift by another. No one can make another human being free." The art of the Third World confronts a system of injustice and oppression that allows some to indulge in extravagant waste while most people are in dire want of food and other necessities. It raises a cry of protest against such a situation, trying to summon human beings to do battle for the creation of their own world and their own freedom.

Notes

1. Rabbi Richard L. Rubinstein, interview comments in "The State of Jewish Belief: A Symposium," *Commentary* 42 (August 1966): 134.

2. Wassily Kandinsky, *Concerning the Spiritual in Art, and Painting in Particular* (New York: George Wittenborn, 1947), pp. 23–24.

3. William Barrett, *Irrational Man: A Study in Existential Philosophy* (New York: Anchor Doubleday Books, 1962), p. 36.

4. Thomas Wolfe, *Look Homeward, Angel* (New York: Charles Scribner's Sons, 1929), p. xix.

5. See Roy McMullen, *Art, Affluence and Alienation* (New York: Praeger, 1968), p. 127.

6. See Florencio Segura, "Teatro y Fe," *Vida Nueva*, March 10, 1973, p. 26.

7. Arthur Miller, *Death of a Salesman*, final scene.

8. A wide variety of dramas rage against marriage as ridiculous (Mihura's *Three Top Hats* and Ionesco's *Jacques ou la soumission*), as a tie that deprives one of liberty, or as mere conventionalism (Mrozek's *Tango*).

9. See Florencio Segura, "Teatro y Fe," p. 31.

10. Leslie Paul, *Alternatives to Christian Belief* (New York: Doubleday, 1967), p. 176.

11. It was some time ago that William Blake pitilessly attacked the disorientation caused by the industrial revolution. In his poetry he expressed the belief that it would "kill man." In his day Baudelaire sought to turn his own poetry into a substitute for religion, into an escape from the positivism and scientism of an age without God.

12. See M. Heidegger, *Being and Time*, Eng. trans. (New York: Harper & Row, 1962), p. 370.

13. León Felipe, *Obras completas* (Buenos Aires: Losada, 1963), p. 121.

14. Ernesto Cardenal, *Salmos* (Buenos Aires: Ed. Carlos Lohlé, 1964), pp. 13–14; Eng. trans.: *Psalms of Struggle and Liberation* (New York: Seabury, 1971). For a good sampling of César Vallejo's work see *Poemas Humanas—Human Poems*, bilingual edition (New York: Grove Press, 1968). More works of Pablo Neruda are also appearing in English at present.

15. In *One Hundred Years of Solitude* loneliness and death are the victors after five generations have passed. Nothing has really changed. José Arcadio Buendía decides that henceforth every day will be Monday. Ursula feels that time has gone round in a circle, that they are back at the beginning again.

16. Faulkner is undoubtedly one of those writers who are most pessimistic about the human condition. *Sanctuary* is a nightmare of evil, and evil seems to be an integral part of human existence in all his work.

17. J. García Hortelano, *El gran momento de Mary Tribune* (Barcelona: Hispánica Nova, Ed. Barral, 1972), pp. 14–15.

18. Only in *The Plague* does Camus suggest rebellion as an answer to the absurd. But as we shall see in a later chapter, it is the absurd that ultimately triumphs.

19. Nausea surrounds Antoine Roquentin in *La nausée*. It is outside him as well as in him, whether he looks in a mirror or at objects in the world.

20. In a similar vein the chief character of Gheorgiu's *The Twenty-Fifth Hour* feels persecuted without knowing the who or why or wherefore. Neither does he know when it will end. He knows nothing at all.

21. Carlos Gurméndez, *El secreto de la alienación* (Barcelona: Ibérica, 1967), p. 198.

22. In this series of anonymous Christs we might include: Joe Christmas in Faulkner's *Light in August,* the old fisherman in Hemingway's *The Old Man and the Sea,* the main characters in A. Schwartz-Bart's *The Last of the Just,* the Christ figure in N. Kazantzakis's *The Greek Passion,* Mauriac's *L'agneau,* and G. Cesbron's *Entre perros y lobos.* There is a whole series of anonymous Christs in contemporary Latin American fiction also. Perhaps the most representative is to be found in Roa Bastos's *Hijo de Hombre.* For further information and details see Edwin Moseley, *Pseudonyms of Christ in the Modern Novel* (Pittsburgh: University of Pittsburgh Press, 1962).

23. "Juan Bonet is preoccupied with little people, with the gray, sensitive human beings who find themselves in a harsh, incomprehensible world. Things happen which they cannot understand. They feel screwed to the wall, and simply keep reciting their own little litany of fantasies" (Antonio Segado del Olmo, in *Reseña,* March 1973, no. 63, p. 17).

24. This terminology is taken from Carlos Fuentes *La nueva novela hispanoamericana* (Mexico City: Joaquín Mortiz, 1969).

25. Ibid., p. 32.

26. Pedro Trigo ("El cristianismo popular en la nueva novela latinoamericana," *SIC* 36, no. 354 [April 1973]: 163–64) brings out this point. It is evident in "the ambiguity shown by the curates in *La feria* when it comes to standing up for the rights of the natives. It is also evident in the ambiguity of the nuns in *La casa verde.* They have a real affection for Bonifacia, . . . but they are also somewhat compliant toward the landowners and authorities who were more or less accomplices in the torture of her father. There is the disembodied spiritualism of the old curate in *Redoble por Rancas,* who is blind to the problem of imperialism and imputes everything to personal sins. There is the harshness of Father García, the curate of Piura, in *La casa verde,* who does not understand the people and chastises them unmercifully. Obsessed with the problem of sexual immorality, he provokes the burning of the house of prostitution and participates in that act. There is the harshness of the priest of Santa María in *Juntacadáveres.* Onetti grants him zeal, right intentions, and an absence of personal animadversions; but for that very reason there is even greater inhumaneness in his implacable crusade against the evil which he sees hypostatized in the little house of prostitution. There is the coarse complicity of the plantation curate with the pitiless military agents of capitalism in *Hijo de Hombre.* More subtle is the association between the landowners and the Father

Director in *Los ríos profundos.* Through his alienating meekness he preaches terrible sermons to the Indians. Of him Arguedas says: "He was intelligent and energetic, but his voice quivered. Centuries of suspicion weighed down on him, and fear, and the thirst to punish" (*Los ríos profundos* [Santiago, Chile: Universitaria, 1967], p. 249). He is the man who comes to punish with the whip the union of the young hero with the people roused to fight for their rights (p. 130).

The tragedy of the curate who is disloyal to his mission appears in its blackest light in *El luto humano* by Revueltas. What was perplexity, sorrow, and impotence in *Al filo del agua* now serves to trigger violence: "He had helped to unleash forces stronger than himself. The power of wrath and of a fierce faith that took control over everything. He was unable to master the violence" (*El luto humano* [Mexico City: Ed. Novero, 1967], p. 281). The embers of hatred still burned in him, . . . and he eventually succumbs. He kills his enemy and loses God, the church, his faith. Like the others, he surrenders to fate, inverting the commandment of love and falling in love with his own death: "What you really love is your own suffering, the tears you are shedding, the entrails within you that are slowly rotting" (*El luto humano*, p. 101). There is nothing left for him to do but to give himself over to death. He thinks about saying some expiatory word, as he thought about it earlier in connection with Ursulo and his companions. But instead he leans back calmly and "disappears in the water" (ibid., p. 121).

27. A growing segment of the clergy is beginning to take cognizance of something that the people of Latin America have always sensed and lived in an obscure way. These clerics are helping to make the point clear to the people in turn. As we shall see further on, this may prove to be the great contribution of liberation theology, which emphasizes the political and liberative core of the Christian faith. Fine expressions of this in fictional form are the curate of *Pedro Páramo*, who joins a group of guerrillas, and the shift to militancy of Father Chacón in *Redoble por Rancas.* When the latter is asked by someone why they have been visited with this punishment from God, the priest replies: "The fence is not the work of God. . . . It is the work of the Americans. It is not enough to pray; one must fight." His people reply that it seems impossible to fight "the Company." The other side controls all the guns, the policemen, and the judges. The priest replies: "Everything is possible with the help of God." They kneel down and ask for his blessing. "Father Chacón made the sign of the cross" (Manuel Scorza, *Redoble por Rancas* [Planeta, 1971], pp. 135–36; Trigo, "Cristianismo popular," p. 165).

28. Leslie Paul, *Alternatives to Christian Belief,* p. 170.

29. See ibid., p. 171.

30. See Richard W. B. Lewis, "The Fiction of Graham Greene: Between the Horror and the Glory," *The Kenyon Review* 19 (Winter 1957): 70–72.

31. See Rollo May, *Love and Will,* Dell paperback edition, pp. 21–23, 316–20.

32. See John Berger, *Success and Failure of Picasso* (Penguin Books, 1969), p. 169. Lorenzo Batallán has this to say about the singular force and power of *Guernica* among Picasso's "distortions": "It is both dreadful and sublime, ferocious and poetic. Not only is it one of man's finest works proclaiming the horror of war; it is also a work of conviction for all history, all the arts, and all civilizations. It is the acme of a dramatic ballet at the silent peak of desolation and death, horror and bloodshed, destruction and absurdity. It is the

apotheosis of catastrophe, the stable where all the horsemen of the Apocalypse have just dismounted, an unredeemed hell without historical or human justification. . . . There is no greater eloquence in art for denunciation, no better proof that one does not need naturalism to capture the most accurate details of reality" (Batallán, "Cuando la inmortalidad es la Patria de un artista; Pablo Picasso," *El Nacional,* Caracas, April 9, 1973).

33. "Death and sex are used to arrive at a conception of agony on the one hand and mockery on the other. They both are linked up with the even more frightening idea that death and coitus are not finished or self-enclosed acts but unsatisfying, interminable situations which resolve nothing. . . . More than anyone else, Bacon fleshes out the existence of modern Europe. It has rejected the notion of transcendence and accepted the relativity of existence, to the point where it now doubts its own sense and meaningfulness. . . . Time involves commitment only in two pragmatic, finalistic actions that end in themselves and leave no traces behind (copulating and dying). . . . Above and beyond his personal situation, his work reveals the situation of a whole civilization. . ." (Marta Traba, "Bacon frente a frente," *Papel Literario/7* of *El Nacional,* Caracas, April 29, 1973).

34. See Roy McMullen, *Art, Affluence and Alienation,* p. 165.

35. See Anthony Padovano, *The Estranged God: Modern Man's Search for Belief* (New York: Sheed and Ward, 1966), p. 184.

36. Ibid., p. 191.

37. Of this film Buñuel said: "It is the only film that tells us, that shows us, what the modern world really signifies." See Carlos Fuentes, "El Discreto Encanto de Luis Buñuel," *El Nacional,* Caracas, April 8, 1973.

38. The works of Dreyer and Bresson are notable exceptions to the general lack of artistic value in most religious films. Carl Dreyer of Denmark presents faith and trust in God as the solution to the chaos and lack of values in the modern world. Among his major films (*The Passion and Death of Joan of Arc, Dies Irae*), the one that stands out is *Ordet* (The Word). It is without a doubt the highest expression of the religious cinema. Of it Fernández-Cuenca writes: "Over against the greatest question-mark in life, the mystery of death, Dreyer sets confidence in God; it is such confidence that can work the miracle of resurrecting the dead. Inger resurrects the love of her own family, but that resurrection does not affect one home alone. It goes on to affect the whole community in which the miracle takes place. What is brought out is a sense of peace and universal brotherhood that can only be obtained through sincere acts of faith" (C. Fernández-Cuenca, "Carl Theodor Dreyer," *Filmoteca Nacional de España,* 1964; taken from Antonio Pelayo, "Cine y Fe," *Vida Nueva,* no. 880, April 28, 1973, p. 26 [640]).

The films of Bresson include *Diary of a Country Priest, The Trial of Joan of Arc, At Random, Balthasar, Mouchette,* and *Four Nights of a Dreamer.* They are a decisive affirmation of the spirit of redemptive sacrifice in the face of a world invaded by sin and evil.

2

PSYCHOLOGY AND DEHUMANIZATION: HUMANKIND TODAY IN THE VIEW OF PSYCHOLOGY

The principal problem of patients today is emptiness.
          —Rollo May
A mass psychology is displacing the individual.
          —Herbert Marcuse

The vision of people today that we have just glimpsed in art is also shared by contemporary psychology. Both psychologists and artists, the people most directly concerned with the human spirit, agree that we are living in an age of anxiety, devaluation, emotional anemia, and "disordered will," to use the expression of Leslie Faber. Psychologists and psychiatrists tell us that human beings today are moving rapidly toward a complete inability to feel authentic feelings, the reification of their affects, and the massification of their will power. Wilhelm Reich referred to modern human beings as "living machines." Erich Fromm talks about "the pathology of normal human beings." Focusing on the identity crisis faced by people today, Erik Erikson suggests that we are moving toward little more than a herd identity. David Riesman presents us as lonely individuals

44

in a lonely crowd. Margaret Mead sees American capitalistic society as the prototype of an inane society. Mills sees it as one big warehouse in which everyone and everything is neatly labelled and manipulated. And Pamela H. Johnson suggests that we may be moving toward a state of complete emotional incapacity.[1]

This emotional anemia and lack of interest in authentic values has led Rollo May to write about "the deep sense of despair and futility which so many people in our day have." They share a condition of "emptiness," which must be taken seriously: "The human being cannot live in a condition of emptiness for very long: if he is not growing *toward* something, he does not merely stagnate; the pent-up potentialities turn into morbidity and despair, and eventually into destructive activities. . . . A human being is not empty in a static sense. . . . The experience of emptiness . . . generally comes from people's feeling that they are *powerless* to do anything effective about their lives or the world they live in."[2]

A sense of futility readily leads to indifference, indifference leads to an inability to love, and this leads to anxiety and neuroticism.[3] Some psychologists do not hesitate to label present-day civilization as neurotic or schizoid. They say that it is totally depersonalized and inauthentic, producing false personalities devoid of will power and the ability to love. In *Modern Man in Search of a Soul,* Carl Gustav Jung noted that more than one-third of his patients were suffering from a kind of neurosis that could not be defined in clinical terms and that was characterized by a feeling of emptiness in their lives. He concluded that it might well be considered the general neurosis of our time.

This pervasive feeling of impotence and meaninglessness is what was called "anomie" by Emile Durkheim. It was discussed in great detail by Wendell Bell, and today it is generally referred to as "alienation."[4] In an earlier day Freud saw the "will to pleasure" (the pleasure principle) as the cure for tensions, and Alfred Adler saw Nietzsche's "will to power," elaborated in psychological terms, as the answer to the same problem. Today psychologists are telling us in all sorts of ways that people really

are searching for meaningfulness rather than power or pleasure. They want something that will give meaning to their lives
and make life itself worth living. When the world and life seem
devoid of meaning, people are invaded by feelings of impotence and uprootedness. Unable to sense their own identity or
to establish authentic relations with others, individuals fall
prey to loneliness and feelings of emptiness. To escape these
feelings, they flee from themselves and immerse themselves in
the anonymous mass.

Modern civilization provides people with plenty of mechanisms for remaining in a state of permanent evasion and
flight. It can convince them that their evil is not evil because it is
shared by all. Thus they are persuaded to avoid the terrible
encounter with self and loneliness that might start them on the
road to an authentic, personal life. Lost in the routine of
monotonous, disembodied work, repeating the slogans they
are told to repeat, using the things that are in vogue and used
by everybody, and sating themselves with the routine, prefabricated pleasure provided by society, people find it impossible
to take cognizance of their most fundamental human desires,
to satisfy their yearning for union and transcendence, and to
explore their own ultimate meaning as human beings.

People today have been turned into isolated pieces in the
mass puzzle. Understanding neither themselves nor others,
they live in solitude in "the lonely crowd." They are strangers
to themselves, to other human beings, to nature, and to the
huge social apparatus that satisfies their material needs while
creating countless others. Their whole way of life is fashioned
for them by that machine. Such beings, Barrett tells us, soon
lose any sense of individual autonomy and begin to equate
themselves with their function in society.[5] When asked who
they are, such people will answer by giving their marital status
or their job description. Status and function provide the only
sense of self that they have. They have no feeling of themselves
as autonomous beings with loves and fears, convictions and
doubts, authentic feelings and desires. It is the social setup that
determines their very being.[6]

Today human beings no longer feel that they are creative

centers of life and existence, that they are in charge of their lives or their possessions. They are isolated atoms in the social structure that people themselves have fashioned. The more powerful the forces that people unleash, the more helpless they feel as individual human beings. Over against their own creations people feel oppressed and dominated by them. They are just other objects without any personal identity.

Such are the human beings we find in the advanced consumerist societies of the capitalist world. Since only objects are appreciated, and since they feel like objects themselves, these human beings tend to identify themselves with their possessions. What they are as human beings is sacrificed to what they have or possess. They recognize themselves only in their objects and their conveniences, as Marcuse has stressed repeatedly. Their identities are bound up with their color TVs and their automobiles, their home furnishings and their wardrobe. They are obsessed with the idea of owning more and better things as they come off the assembly line. This is their dominant concern, their one and only dimension, for they know that their culture will judge their stature in those terms. They are more respectable, more dignified, if they drive the latest model car and belong to the best clubs. To have or own what is in vogue is their great yearning and only aim. Yet under the accumulated mass of things lies a great personal emptiness.

Since their work routine and their passionate quest for possessions does not give them satisfaction, people today unconsciously repress their feelings of desperation and emptiness by submitting to the routine of prepackaged entertainment and pleasure. The pleasure industry provides them with sounds and pictures, products and bodies. So we are drawing closer and closer to the image that Aldous Huxley drew in *Brave New World* (1932): a creature who is well fed, well dressed, and sexually satisfied, but who is devoid of depth, identity, and the possibility of communicating with others. They are directed by superficial slogans that have the force of law. They promise fulfillment to everyone. They try to assure people that they have everything they need to live authentic lives. They try to get people to live from moment to moment, without exploring anything too deeply or getting greatly concerned about anything. Honor and distinction are to be found in doing what everyone else does. There is no room for unhappiness because one has everything one needs—except the ability to make decisions, a sense of community, a concern for others, personalist depth, and the ability to make real commitments.

Thus day-to-day life is robbed of all real value. It is dedicated to the pursuit of material comfort alone, to the production and consumption of things. No value is worthwhile or serviceable if it cannot be measured and quantified and sold in the marketplace. People are neurotic, unbalanced, subversive if they choose to work on the basis of ideals or personal inclinations, if they refuse to follow in the footsteps of everyone else. We are content to live in an inane world, convinced that our happiness will increase the more we immerse ourselves in its monotonous routine, its stress on owning things, and its prefabricated pleasures. [7]

In short, people go through life carrying strangers inside themselves. Caught up in the routines and mechanisms of society, they refuse to pay any consideration to their life, their destiny, and its possible meaning.

In countless ways the mass media of deculturalization cater to the need for fantasy and escape. Terrified to confront ourselves, we need only flick a switch or play a record to escape into an artificial world of sounds and images. Even sleeping and waking are rendered passive by the news or the music coming in over the clock-radio. People are terrified when they contemplate the idea of sitting without talking, drinking, reading, listening to music, or watching TV. The very idea of being alone with oneself makes a person nervous.

For Heidegger silence is part of the personal rhythm of human life. It is the place where one encounters self and explores the deeper levels of meaningfulness. For Whitehead and Tillich it is a necessity for dialogue and prayer. Yet we avoid silence like the plague. We have created a whole world of noises to escape from it. As Max Picard sees it, the miracle of modern technology has been employed chiefly to eliminate silence and thus to prevent our encounter with self. [8]

Such is the picture of the modern human being: alienated from self, others, and nature; lost in the anonymity of a lonely crowd and the din of all sorts of noises; incapable of deeper feelings and riddled with feelings of anxiety, guilt, and insecurity.[9] He is Jaspers's sophist, Mills's fixist, Marcuse's one-dimensional man, Riesman's lonely being, Erikson's conformist, Arnold Green's child of the middle class, and Ortega's mass-man. In those rare moments of real sincerity, these people suddenly realize that they have lost their identity, that they are automatons, that they are neurotic and no longer know how to love.[10]

Modern society promises happiness for all, but it is an empty mass happiness without any depth of feeling. Modern society is destroying our capacity for authentic love. Surrounded by things and possessions, we are losing our capacity for self-determination, freedom, and commitment. Caught up in the pursuit of promised pleasures, we are egotists closed up in ourselves and devoid of any capacity for love. Heidegger has suggested that a basic concern for others (*Sorge*) is one of the essential constituents of a truly human existence. Thus we seem to be faced with human beings who are now living an inhuman existence. Erich Fromm suggests that human beings are used by others for the sake of power and pleasure or else they use themselves for their own power and pleasure; in either case human beings become nothing more than means toward merely material ends. In past centuries inhuman behavior meant cruelty and slavery. In today's consumerist world, suggests Fromm, it primarily means massification, the loss of individual personality, an inability to love, and herd-life.[11]

Notes

1. Over against this humanist psychology opposing the system there stands another, of course. It is the false, dehumanizing psychology which supports totalitarian planning and proposes personal "adjustment" as the answer for the tensions of people today. Individuals must adapt to the norms and principles voiced by the system's spokespeople. Examples of this antihumanism would be the work of McKinney, the writings of Dale Carnegie, and others of

that sort. Basically they suggest that happiness and success are to be found by blindly following the depersonalized norms imposed by some outside authority or computer.

2. Rollo May, *Man's Search for Himself* (New York: W.W. Norton & Company, 1953), pp. 14, 24–25.

3. There is Melvin Seeman's work on alienation in a mass society, whose broad lines have now been accepted by many psychologists and sociologists. (See Melvin Seeman, "El estudio de la alienación en la sociedad de masas," *La alienación como concepto sociológico,* Spanish edition [Buenos Aires: Signos, 1970]). Seeman points up five essential features of a mass-based society: impersonal relationships, secularization, heterogeneity, mobility, and increased size. In the individual they produce feelings of powerlessness, meaninglessness, normlessness, value isolation, and self-estrangement. In short, we get a confused and disoriented life, which is totally dehumanized and lacks meaning and purpose.

4. Marx was one of the first to explore the concept of human alienation in depth and to describe its impact on people as workers. Forced to sell their labor power and unable to benefit from its fruits, people cannot carry out the process of becoming human beings. In present-day society laborers work for a wage. They are not the owners of the product of their work, so work alienates and dehumanizes them instead of helping them to attain human fulfillment: "The object produced by his labor . . . stands over against him as an alien entity. . . . The laborer invests his life in the object; his life comes to belong to the object rather than to himself. The greater his activity is, the less he possesses and has to show for it. What is incorporated into the product of his labor is no longer his. The greater his production is, the more he himself is diminished. The alienation of the worker in the product of his work means that the product is turned into something not only external but also hostile to him. The life which he gave to the object is turned against him as an alien and hostile force" (See Karl Marx, *Early Writings* [New York: McGraw-Hill, 1964], p. 122, for this passage).

A necessary consequence of this alienation in work is religious alienation. Because people do not find self-satisfaction in their work, they imagine another world where fulfillment is to be found. They escape to an illusory world because they cannot find security and happiness in this world. These ideas will be considered in greater detail in Chapter 9.

In his *History and Class Consciousness* (Eng. trans., Cambridge, Mass.: MIT Press, 1971), György Lukacs pushed the Marxist study of alienation further. He described the "mystification" practiced in the capitalist world. Transposing the division of labor into the ethical sphere, it makes alienation itself sacred. This is evident in the capitalistic stress on bureaucratic integrity and objectivity, total submissiveness to bureaucratic demands, and the equation of a sense of responsibility and productivity with obedience at work. Thus consciousness is further reified, and as such it becomes a basic category of societal life.

Mannheim's work on alienation is also of interest here. He describes two interconnected phases of it, its objective and subjective sides. On the objective side people are deprived of freedom and initiative, and hence subjected to total impotence. On the subjective side individuals cannot comprehend the laws governing the mechanisms in which they participate. Giuseppe Bonazzi studied the subjective phase of alienation among a group of workers in a Fiat plant. He concluded that when people must live in a state of objective alienation, they are not personally conscious of it and so suffer from subjective alienation as well (G. Bonazzi, "Alienazione e anomia tra i lavorari della Fiat: Risultati di une indagine sociologica," in *Tempi Moderni,* January-March 1963, No. 12, pp. 9–44).

Today alienation is usually understood in a broader sense as the condition of people characterized by meaninglessness, disorientation, dehumanization, loss of interest, and emotional impotence. Anthony Davids described it as a psychological syndrome with the following characteristics: a tendency toward egocentrism, mistrust, pessimism, anxiety, and resentment. See his article, "Alienation, Social Apperception, and Ego Structures," *Journal of Consulting Psychology* 19 (1955): 21–27.

5. William Barrett, *Irrational Man: A Study in Existential Philosophy* (New York: Doubleday Anchor Books, 1962), p. 31.

6. See Erich Fromm, *The Sane Society* (New York: Fawcett World Library, 1967), Chapter 5.

7. All this was seen earlier by Pascal. He noted that people were trying to evade encounter with self through routine and diversion. This was a suicidal course, concealing from people their nothingness, emptiness, and impotence.

8. See Max Picard, *The Flight from God* (Chicago: Regnery, 1951), p. 1.

9. See Barry McLaughlin, *Nature, Grace and Religious Development,* (Westminster, Md.: Newman Press, 1964), p. 3.

10. See Erich Fromm, *The Art of Loving* (New York: Harper & Row, 1956).

11. See Erich Fromm, *You Shall Be as Gods* (New York: Fawcett World Library, 1969), p. 48; idcm, *The Sane Society.*

3

THE ATHEISTIC
CIVILIZATION

*Atheism is not something superficial, a passing fad. It is a
sign of the times embodying a new situation for humanity
in both subjective and objective terms. Thus it is leaving a
profound imprint on the present, even as it will have the
same impact on the future.*

—Giulio Girardi

The civilization I have been describing above is totally
materialistic and dedicated to the production and enjoyment
of things. It is grounded on the principles of egotism, individualism, and exploitation; and it supports an inane, mass-
based culture that places severe restrictions on all personal
decision-making. Such a civilization is clearly an atheistic one.
Or to be more accurate, it is an idolatrous civilization, as we
shall see.

When people talk about atheistic materialism, they generally
think only about the communist world, which has abolished
God from its culture by decree. They seldom realize that the
technocratic culture of mass consumption is essentially materialistic and atheistic as well. It, too, has suppressed God
and alienated religion—not by decree but by fostering a lifestyle that is radically opposed to any authentic religion. A
system that nurtures herds of human begins who obey without

being subjected to force, who are directed by slogans and television commercials, who live as machines and passively enjoy their possessions without showing any personality or freedom of their own, and who erect their little whiff of power on the exploitation of whole peoples, is clearly an atheistic system even though it may inscribe the name of God in gold letters in its Constitution.

In such a world religion is tolerated only if it serves as just another routine, only if it aids and abets the mechanisms of the system that turn people into anonymous masses. If religion recovers its liberative mission, it is sure to be persecuted. The God accepted and worshipped in such a system is an idol. He is the God who stands for dominion and paternalism, the God who guarantees tranquility amid oppression and alienation, the shadowy God way up there who has given his blessing to the mechanisms and delights of the system. There is really no room for a God who stands for human liberation, who loves justice and freedom, who forces people to be fully human.

This being the case, we are confronted with a paradox that we shall consider in greater detail further on. In such a situation atheism may actually be the rejection of false notions of God. It may actually represent a real form of solid faith. On the other hand a self-satisfied faith devoid of any humanizing practice may actually serve as a cover for a radical atheism.

Thus it should not surprise us to find that atheism is endemic to the alienating culture of the consumerist world. As Martin Marty points out, one of the most striking features of modern atheism is its widespread diffusion. It seems bound to become as widespread as the air we breathe.[1] Only on an atheistic foundation can we maintain our inhuman world of today. It matters little that people continue to maintain that they believe in God. They say that out of habit, or because they do not really know what they are saying. In fact their lives are completely atheistic, grounded on principles that categorically rule out any sound comprehension of God.

Today atheism is no longer an articulated ideology as it may have been in the last century. Instead it is a way of life, the foundation on which our modern world and our western civilization is built. As Jean Lacroix suggested, it is the starting point for a new way of living rather than the conclusion of a reasoned argument.[2]

Let us face up to the situation courageously, eschewing all attempts at childish escapism. In our world today atheism is the normal situation for the depersonalized masses. Many people, those who are most consistent and logical, admit that they are "natural atheists," and that they have a positive distaste for those zealous believers who would turn them into "anonymous Christians." In many instances their atheism is radical and total; they do not care one whit about God, and they feel no need to offer a logical justification for their attitude. The existence or nonexistence of God is a matter of no importance whatsoever. It is not worth troubling about, and it will not change things one bit in any case. Believers and nonbelievers both meet with success and failure, triumph and defeat, and death. Faith offers no real help at all. If believers are sick and want to get well, they must resort to a doctor even though they may claim to place their hope in God. And in fact their real-life hopes for the future are based on their money, their foresight, and their securities rather than on any faith in divine providence.

People today substantiate Bonhoeffer in asserting that they have learned to face up to important questions without having any recourse to God. The real problem is that people are not capable of believing in a God who is not constantly intervening in human affairs. Modern culture is not interested in a God who does not step in clearly and forthrightly on humanity's side, who has been supplanted by science and no longer seems to be of any use. Today truth is what works in favor of people; other sorts of value judgments are often considered to be little more than poor syntax. When human beings in such a culture begin to feel their contingency, anxiety, and radical finiteness, they seek to allay such feelings by scouring the landscape for power, prestige, pleasure or, in the case of the most generous-hearted, by trying to construct a more just and humane world.

God is beginning to disappear completely from the world.

Fewer and fewer people are looking to God for the final, definitive response to their condition and the unanswered question it poses. Fewer and fewer people are living their faith in God as a concrete praxis of commitment to the world and other people. When we hear the name of God spoken in our culture, it sounds like something fictitious. Many people, including believers, are ashamed to bring up God's name in public or to declare their faith in God openly.

Today it is true that modern atheism has many features and facets. Faith and atheism are existential decisions, fundamental options freely made by the individual. Hence they are singular in each case. Yet we can increasingly detect a common denominator in modern atheism: i.e., its complete silence about, and total lack of interest in, everything having to do with God and religion. It is a depersonalized phenomenon of masses as everything else is. Even when people profess faith in God, they are atheists in the same sense that they think they are free in choosing between all the products that are forced on them, or happy by doing everything they are told to do in order to be happy. Atheism has ceased to be merely an ideology and has become a basic attitude of life.

People today are no longer hostile to God or religion, no longer look for arguments to refute them. People simply are not interested. Vahanian suggests that the post-Christian person "simply does not raise the religious question at all, not even in church."[3] Erich Fromm puts it this way: "The majority of us believe in God, take it for granted that God exists. The rest, who do not believe, take it for granted that God does not exist. Either way, God is taken for granted. Neither belief nor disbelief cause any sleepless nights, nor any serious concern. In fact, whether a man in our culture believes in God or not makes hardly any difference either from a psychological or from a truly religious standpoint. In both instances he does not care—either about God or about the answer to the problem of his own existence."[4] This silence about God in our conversation and activities reveals people's total lack of interest in everything having to do with religion. They have moved from hostility to total indifference. This is the atheism that typifies the depersonalized masses. They accept only the tangible, material, consumable values of the macro-system based on production and consumption.

Aware of the general diffusion of atheism and its impact even on the lives of believers, atheists themselves tend to view it as a necessary process of historical maturation. Its successful outcome will be only a matter of time, in their view. Some day universal atheism will be a reality pointing to the full and complete maturity of *homo sapiens*. Julian Huxley writes that our advancing scientific knowledge has rendered the idea of God obsolete. The Christian faith has nothing worthwhile to offer people insofar as their future development is concerned. Following the lines of Comte, Huxley tries to show that such ideas as magic, spirit, and God are outmoded, belonging to the past and the undeveloped state of science of an earlier day. God must soon disappear from the scene of history altogether, since the gods were mere ideas and symbols. To grant them objective existence is to reinstate the reign of superstition, whose guardian is the church. To prevent this, we must establish a humanist religion with its own rites and symbols. Continued belief in God is inexcusable because it is a clear sign of impotence and a lack of confidence in human power.[5]

To the spokespeople of modern atheism faith in God is something that belongs to the past and that is on its way out. In *Science and Religion* Whitehead notes that the religious question continues to show a decline in interest. In his book *Suicide* Durkheim talked about "the ruins of ancient beliefs." Huxley, Fromm, and others propose some of atheistic, humanist religion to fill the void created by the now defunct idea of God. Concern about God, even talk about God, is considered to be unscientific, mythological, obsolete. What had been associated with God is not sufficiently explained by science, psychology, sociology, and history.

The most convinced atheists feel they need not expend energy attacking the remaining traces of belief in God. Such a policy would be counterproductive anyway. It would only stimulate believers to organize their fantasies better. Persecution would only reinforce them in their ideas. It is better to let the idea of God disappear naturally as the sciences move toward complete victory and as people fully discover their own worth and dignity. The remaining vestiges of religion can be disregarded because they have lost all force and vitality.

There is no need to attack the idea of God, suggests Maurice Nadeau. Today the world is not influenced at all by religion. It does not matter at all that the laborer and his boss are Christians who go to the same church, for it is in the factory that they live their real lives and faith has no influence there. There is no need to talk or worry about God and religion. Those subjects no longer have any influence on real life. They retain only a social dimension that does harm to no one. Some people go to church as others go to their private clubs. The vestiges of cultural and social custom demand that children be baptized in some places, that they get married or buried according to certain rites. But there is no longer anything deeply religious in these practices. Belief and nonbelief do not change anything in the life of human beings. Even the mass of believers live as if God did not exist. As Paul Ramsey suggests, our culture today is the first to operate on the premise that God is dead.

To be sure, we cannot ignore the fact that many people today continue to profess faith in God. They would categorically deny that they are atheists. But in most instances faith is merely a word used to cover the radical atheism of their practical, everyday lives. They regard faith simply as something that has to be believed, not as a basic attitude that must be translated into concrete action in their lives. God is accepted as something or someone who guarantees their atheistic way of life. For them religion has completely lost its critical sense. It is an opiate that reinforces the meaninglessness of an inhuman world and its mechanisms.

People claim to believe in God, but their God is an idol who sanctions and safeguards the power and framework of their culture, a culture based upon the suffering and blood of whole peoples. He is the God of the white conqueror, the God who expects submission from those who are enslaved, the God who is invoked by the oppressors against the dawning consciousness of the poor and oppressed, the God of the colonizers who denies humanity and equality to the colonized. People feel happier and more secure with this God at their side. They are convinced that he will guarantee and support the power and authority of their elected officials against the inroads of Communists and atheists. This same God is even supported by the system itself, because he helps to keep the masses tame and herd-like. Besides, he doesn't ask for much: a few prayers, a few religious practices, and perhaps a few alms now and again. In return he offers affluence here and an eternity of happiness hereafter. Surely it is obvious that such a faith, which uses God to maintain an inhuman world, is far more harmful than any declared atheism.

Other masses of people, particularly in Latin America, live lives that stand in marked contrast to the declared atheism of some and the tacit atheism of consumerist society. They are living lives of deeply rooted, unshakeable faith. Christianity has become an inseparable part of their culture and their lives. Their religiosity is often denigrated by the oppressor oligarchy, by theoretical believers, and by theologies of the prevailing system. It is often called superstition, magic, idolatry, and so forth. But as Enrique Dussel points out, there is real faith in this religiosity: faith in the poor person one is and in the other poor people around. It is not any sort of conscious knowledge or doctrine. Rather "it is *a capacity to believe,* an openness to the eschatological order because one does not believe in the existing order. . . . Poor people believe and trust in the poor. That is why they are open to the poor man of Nazareth and can believe in the revelation of the absolute Other . . . who has nothing to do with the total system that now prevails: the system of capitalism that now prevails in dependent Latin America."[6]

The people of Latin America are a Christian people. They have faith. Their faith may be a bit confused, interlarded with elements that have to be purified. But they do believe deeply in a God who loves them and wants their liberation, who is felt to be close to them and to whom they can entrust their suffering and their misery. At the same time they live their faith as a sincere practice of service toward others, who are just as downtrodden and oppressed as they are. The people of Latin America feel that God is with them in the new Christ who continues to be crucified *en masse* by the agents of the oppressing system. The people of Latin America hope in their God with open hearts, knowing that he shared their sorrow in order to bring complete and definitive liberation to the world. The response to atheism will not come from the theologies fabricated in the world of the oppressor. In the last analysis such theologies only help to foster the atheization of an inhuman world. The response will come from the Christianity of these poor people who are experiencing the nearness of God in their service to their fellows. As I see it, and as I shall discuss later on, this is the great contribution of the theology of liberation. It sees faith as a praxis that liberates people from every sort of oppression. It liberates people from economic, social, political, and ideological oppression. It liberates people from the idol that they have made of themselves. It opens people to the possibility of a sound and sane acceptance of God because "faith is possible only if one is atheistic with regard to oneself."[7]

Notes

1. See Martin Marty, *Varieties of Unbelief* (New York: Holt, Rinehart & Winston, 1964).

2. Jean Lacroix, *The Meaning of Modern Atheism,* Eng. edition (Dublin: Gill, 1965), p. 81.

3. Gabriel Vahanian, *The Death of God: The Culture of Our Post-Christian Era* (New York: G. Braziller, 1961), p. 148.

4. Erich Fromm, *The Sane Society* (New York: Holt, Rinehart & Winston, 1955), p. 176.

5. See Julian Huxley, *The Humanist Frame* (London: Allen & Unwin, 1961), pp. 14, 42, 49, and passim.

6. Enrique Dussel, *America Latina: Dependencia y liberación* (Buenos Aires: Cambeiro, 1973), p. 215.

7. Ibid., p. 202.

4

THE NEW ABSOLUTES: THE INVASION OF IDOLATRY

A rain of gods descends from heaven on the funeral rites of the one unique God who outlived himself. Now atheists have their saints and blasphemers are building chapels.
—Leszek Kolakowski

Having rejected God, we have enthroned the products of our own hand on the vacant altars and now kneel in adoration before them. The rejection of God has led to a "flood of idolatry" (Bossuet) that now covers the face of the earth. Thus our new civilization is not so much atheistic as idolatrous, and the new false gods leave people with empty hearts. Having embraced our new idols, we find our lives and all meaningfulness slipping away. We live amid the crushing tension created by emptiness on the one hand and anxious searching on the other. We slew God in order to be more fully human; then we surrendered our hearts to idols that have dehumanized him. Only now, in the throes of our new bondage, can we begin to realize that only God can liberate us from our new deities, that only God deserves our heartfelt surrender and can offer any perduring surety for our humanism.

Since God is a hidden God, idolatry always remain our great

temptation. Even believers will continue to be attracted to it because we need something tangible on which to pin our hopes. As Vahanian has pointed out, human beings have always tended toward idolatry whether they were religious or not. The tendency is so strong that they would invent a god if God did not exist. Even if God does exist, human beings are willing to kill him in order to justify their idolatry in the face of the ambiguities posed by life and their own behavior.[1]

Mircea Eliade assures us that the completely areligious human being is an extremely rare phenomenon, even in the most desacralized forms of modern society. Even those who are atheists in practice retain all sorts of camouflaged myths, debased rituals, and superstitions. Societal celebrations and family festivities frequently display religious aspects:

> But it is not only in the "little religions" or in the political mystiques that we find degenerated or camouflaged religious behavior. It is no less to be seen in movements that openly avow themselves to be secular or even antireligious. Examples are nudism or the movements for complete sexual freedom. . . . From one point of view it could almost be said that in the case of those moderns who proclaim that they are nonreligious, religion and mythology are "eclipsed" in the darkness of their unconscious—which means too that in such men the possibility of reintegrating a religious view of life lies at a great depth. Or . . . it could also be said . . . that nonreligious man has lost the capacity to live religion consciously, and hence to understand and assume it; but that, in his deepest being, he still retains a memory of it. . . .[2]

Thus it seems that it is very difficult for human beings to live without worshipping something. If they do not worship God, then they will worship nature, or technology, or the idols of the movie and sports world, or their party, or themselves and their own personal ideas. Atheism and idolatry are inseparable. A false conception of God leads to atheism, but atheism in turn gives rise to new forms of idolatry. People reject God because God seems useless or an obstacle to human greatness; then they give their hearts to the petty gods that give life and entertainment to their new culture. A host of idols rise out of the tomb of the dead God, capturing the hearts of dehumanized human beings who regard themselves as atheists.

The Divinization of Science and the Machine

At first science simply sought to get beyond God. At a more advanced stage, however, it has ended up taking God's place. Science itself is now the new deity that explains everything. It has rendered the hypothesis of God obsolete and superfluous. Now it offers us a whole constellation of lesser deities—machines and objects—and we in turn surrender our hearts to them with all the passion we possess. Faith, hope, and charity have not disappeared from the modern world; they have simply taken a new turn. Now human beings have blind faith in what the scientists and technicians tell them. In them they place their hopes for a better and more humane future. And all their love is directed toward the realm of machines that will ensure them convenience and pleasure and which are perfected more and more every day by science.

But while science has played an important role in the atheization of the contemporary world, it is clear that its true mission was meant to be a liberating one. Instead of acting as a substitute for religion, science was meant to purify it. Science opened up new horizons, giving us a new view of our relationship with nature and the world. The present life is not simply a passing stage in a journey to the hereafter, nor is it simply a test to which we must submit before attaining another life beyond the grave. It is not a regimen of order and power to which we should passively submit. This world itself, it turns out, is the place where our complete fulfillment is to be realized. It is both an invitation and a challenge, summoning us to employ our human creativity to the utmost. Nature must be tamed, sources of energy must be brought under control, and raw materials must be used to benefit and serve human life.

We are no longer prompted by natural ignorance or piety to leave things as we have found them, to avoid all that is hostile or disagreeable, or to appeal to divine intervention in the face of a savagely cruel nature. Our activity in the world is not marked by meek resignation to the natural order of things. Instead we seek to transform and order the natural world, to bring it under our control and make it convivial. We know that we dominate and control the world, indeed to the point where we could bring it all to an end.

There can be no doubt about the positive and liberating role of science when it is properly employed. It certainly can and does liberate us from the harsh conditionings of nature, and only science makes it possible for macro-humanity to enjoy a dignified and pleasant lifestyle. It can also liberate us by helping to keep faith on the right track. Science has made it possible for us to come closer to authentic knowledge of God. As Lacroix put it, we cannot give the name "God" to anything that science encounters. It has liberated us from countless idols in the course of human history, from things which we had taken to be God. We should be grateful to science, as Sertillanges points out, because it has forced us to abandon our worship of the sun god, the sky god, the dragon god of eclipses, and all sorts of religious bagatelles.[3]

It is quite obvious that in the past science has done much to preserve the purity of authentic faith, and that it can and should continue to play that role in the present and the future. Today we know that neither the world nor anything mundane or material can be God. Today we realize, more than ever before, that God can never be an object of scientific investigation or experimentation since God transcends those fields. Strictly speaking, science cannot be theistic or atheistic; it should maintain neutrality between those alternatives. If it adheres to its principles and its methods, then it cannot arrive at any conclusion affirming or denying an Absolute.[4] If scientific investigation comes across some being and calls it "God," that being can only be an idol. Proving the existence of God scientifically would come down to objectifying and materializing God. If God is to remain God, then he must ever remain hidden from the reaches of scientific experimentation. He is not a being open to experimental research; he is the reason behind all being, the ultimate foundation of all that exists.[5]

But science was dazzled by its own powers and achievements. Going beyond its mission and its methodological exigencies, it laid down a doctrinal affirmation: If God cannot be experienced by science and is unnecessary for scientific work, then God does not exist.[6] Closing its mind to any knowledge that lay beyond the boundaries of scientific methodology and experimentation, science refused to acknowledge any being that did not reveal its pragmatic usefulness. Thus it "scientized" the human outlook, rejecting all thinking that is not analytic or experimental.[7] A reality that cannot be experienced by science and its methodology is simply no reality at all. A being of no usefulness is also of no real interest.

Thus enslaved to science and tangible experience, we have capitulated to our own humanism.[8] God is rejected as an atavistic vestige of outmoded cultures, as obsolete and of no relevance for human wellbeing (Huxley). Interest in God is to be reserved for the specialist in mythology or the historian of past cultures. Some day God will disappear once and for all from the earth even as earlier mythological figures have done. That is God's fate. In the primitive stages of history humankind needed that illusion; now that we have come of age, we can cast aside God because we no longer need him. It is science that tells us what we are to believe and that explains all that is explicable.

Taking this distorted view, the scientific mentality reduced everything to numbers and measurement, accepting only what is useful and quantifiable. This inevitably led to the complete triumph of technocracy. The human subject has been fitted into some neat pigeonhole, humanity has been turned into an anonymous herd, and the machine has been deified.

People created machines to satisfy their needs. Today the machine has become their greatest need. This machine-laden world is not one of freedom but one of the most deep-rooted and painful bondage. Some years ago Marcel noted that technocratic societies are characterized by an "astonishing sadness" because they mutilate humanism and the human personality, because human beings gradually lose their identity in them and become little more than a herd. Today it is the machine that commands and we who obey. It molds new personalities and creates its own realm of values. Deluded by our scientific power, we rejected God and now live a new form of alienation. We are now enslaved to the new gods of science and the machine, which have not liberated us at all.

God commissioned us to take charge of the world and humanize it. He made us the absolute rulers over nature, animals, and things. God implanted a controlling intelligence in us so that we might transform nature into a realm in our own service. Now we have reversed those roles, surrendering to the enticement of our own creations and thereby allowing things to command a dehumanized humanity.

The Divinization of Sex

This atomistic and depersonalized lifestyle grounded on objects and machines gives rise to feelings of loneliness and anxiety. It leads us to an unconscious yearning for union with others. Shaken by the abyss of emptiness that lies before us, we yearn to participate in some deeper relationship that will give us satisfaction and fulfillment, that will reveal to us our being and our value. Usually we try to overcome our loneliness through some form of love, for unconsciously we realize that our salvation lies in some sort of contact and encounter.

Today, however, love is one of the things that is downgraded and manipulated most in this world of consumerism. We are led to confuse love with possessiveness. Succumbing to the idolatry of sex as technique, we find ourselves even more disoriented, insecure, and famished. An obsession with sex characterizes our technocratic world, pervading the media of communication and entertainment. According to psychologists, this obsession with sex does not just help people to feel some sense of life and personal importance; it also enables them to repress and evade their fear of death.

Rollo May suggests that this tendency to repress death has a history behind it. When the idea of immortality faded out in the eighteenth and nineteenth century, people repressed the thought of death with their faith in progress. Humankind would conquer nature, eliminate every disease, and perhaps eventually manage to overcome death itself. This triumphalist scientific optimism of an earlier day gave way when people experienced the negative, corrupting power of badly used science and their own intrinsic limits. Science did not bring about liberation; instead it created a world marked by monotony and tediousness. That is why sex has moved to the forefront today, replacing progress as one of the main values in modern culture.

In the eyes of people like Tolstoy and Heidegger, confronting the radical possibility of death marks the beginning of any authentic life. It is only then that we will begin to live out our most fundamental plans and projects, abandoning all that is superficial and vacuous. Plato noted that life is an apprenticeship for dying, that death is the essential act of our life and should not be endured passively. We must wait for it and receive it with our eyes and hearts open. For Christian asceticism death has always served as a springboard toward generosity and authentic living insofar as it underlined the fleeting nature of everything terrestrial and prompted human beings to trust themselves to the real author of life. We find the same vein of thought in Leonardo Da Vinci, who saw death as complete rest from a lifetime of work. He took delight in the thought of death as the hard laborer takes delight in the thought of a night's rest. For the mystics, death is their boon companion, the beginning of complete fulfillment, happiness, and peace. They, like Saint Theresa, "die for want of dying."

When human beings face up to their own death, they take their life and being in their hands and set off on their true course. In today's scientific culture, however, people are always fleeing from themselves and neurotically trying to evade all thought of *their own* death. Realizing that they cannot eliminate death, they have decided not to think about it at all, as Pascal once noted. Our machine-age civilization greatly abets this flight and repression. The presence of death is rarely noticed today. Or when it is noticed, it is presented in a sensationalist, depersonalized way that remains remote and abstract. All the emphasis is on life, success, and the pursuit of happiness.[9] And when people are forced to think of death, an air of comedy surrounds the whole funeral scene. Esthetic surgery and cosmetics pretty up the corpse to look beautiful, inoffensive, and unreal. Beautifully dressed and surrounded by flowers, the corpse does not seem to be dead at all. Looking at a corpse in a funeral parlor, few people are inclined to ponder death as serious and definitive. Psychologists for the prevailing system even urge people not to think of death at all. Life is wonderful, they suggest. Why think about death? This repression of death is bound to appear in other sorts of manifestations. Today it has given rise to the "fascism of sex." We live in a world of pansexualism. Sex dominates our thinking, our yearning, and the realm of publicity. Today it has become our most important value. All the problems of the individual are reduced to their sexual adequateness or inadequateness. Books, magazines, films, lecturers, and medical experts promise complete happiness to those who master the proper sexual techniques. Psychologists like Sorokin propose to measure human personality in terms of sex, others propose pleasure as an ethical norm, and still others would base morality on statistics. Kinsey, for example, "argues that right and wrong are not his business. He is simply a scientific reporter who is trying to find out what goes on. But he carries to great lengths the syllogism that (1) man is an animal; (2) some animals do all the things that are condemned in modern society as abnormal or perverted; (3) since animals are natural, this behavior is natural."[10]

Thus sex has become one of the major deities. It gives people a feeling of being alive, proves that they are still young and good for something. For a few moments people can escape the condition of nonbeing that seems to affect the mass man. As Riesman puts it:

Sex, therefore, provides a kind of defense against the threat of total apathy. This is one of the reasons why so much excitement is channelled into sex by the other-directed person. He looks to it for reassurance that he is alive. . . . The other-directed person looks to sex not for display but for a test of his or her ability to attract, his or her place in the "rating-dating" scale—and beyond that, in order to experience life and love.[11]

In full flight from self and caught in a blind search for fulfillment, we seek to escape the abyss of our own meaninglessness by indulging in sex. It is there that we will find proof that our being and our life are important. Caught between the desire for adventure and the snares of illusion, we live out an erotic fantasy that is greatly nourished by a culture based on convenience and pleasure. Whereas past generations came to regard desexualized love as the ideal, this generation seeks sex for its own sake, sex without love.

Amid this erotic frenzy, however, we are beginning to realize that sex can never be an end in itself, that it is burdensome and disappointing if it is not integrated with authentic love. When sexual libertinism itself leads to weariness and nausea, then people look to other forms of escape in drugs and hallucinogens. The god of sex does not bring liberation either; it brings only loathing and another form of bondage. Those who idolize sex live in a state of permanent obsession that becomes more and more empty and unsatisfying.

The Religion of Consumption

We could go on reciting an endless list of the new idols in modern technocratic and capitalistic civilization. It grooms countless heroes and deities to win the hearts of the masses. I refer to the endless series of stars and heroes who occupy center stage in the world of stage, screen, song, sports, television, and theater. They are the false gods erected by mass culture, and to them the public build shrines and offer their admiration. Catching a glimpse of one's hero and receiving an autographed picture become absolute experiences fraught with meaningfulness amid the monotonous round of an otherwise colorless life. The masses yearn for contact with their idols, if only on the television screen. It is a new way of experiencing the "numinous," carefully laid out and promoted by agents, promoters, and the media for sales promotion.

We would also have to mention the new political gods, the parties and candidates in which people invest belief and which they then follow irrationally. Though our technocratic world has allegedly undermined the foundations of all faith, it has somehow managed to produce people who will follow their leaders anywhere, blindly accepting and believing all they say and promise.

We also should mention the new god, money. Money is

omnipotent and irresistible. It can work magic and miracles. Not only is money itself divine, it also divinizes its possessors and makes them omnipotent.[12]

But I think enough has been said to bring out the idolatrous nature of our machine-age culture of the masses. Gods are continually being created and re-created in the orgiastic religion of consumerism. Things, objects, idols, and persons are devoured and consumed. The communications media and the entertainment media—the priests and overseers of the new religion—have taken on the task of drugging the populace. The people must go on believing that they are happy and special because they use a certain brand of soap or eat a certain brand of hot dogs. In fact, however, it all comes down to consumption of one sort or another:

Man's happiness today consists in "having fun." Having fun lies in the satisfaction of consuming and "taking in" commodities, sights, food, drinks, cigarettes, people, lectures, books, movies—all are consumed, swallowed. The world is one great object for our appetite, a big apple, a big bottle, a big breast; we are the suckler, the eternally expectant ones, the hopeful ones—and the eternally disappointed ones. Our character is geared to exchange and to receive, to barter and to consume; everything, spiritual as well as material objects, becomes an object of exchange and of consumption.[13]

We now have new saints to imitate, new ideals to follow in our dehumanized world. The holy ones are the people who possess more and consume more, who trade in their cars every year, spend their summer at the most exotic beaches, dress in the very latest fashions. God is dead in the life of this culture. Now wedded to our new idols and caught up in the frenzy of our new religion, we are beginning to agonize over our situation just a bit. Perhaps only God, the liberator God, can really save us.

From Weariness to Denunciation and Annunciation

Having taken note of our new bondage, we are now beginning to resolve firmly to liberate ourselves. More and more people, particularly young people, are rejecting a world based

on alienation and oppression. They want to commit themselves to the task of creating a very different world, a world
based on justice and liberty.

The groups and movements involved in this new course are
very different and sometimes even diametrically opposed to
each other. What they share with each other is their opposition
to, and rejection of, the values and lifestyle that their own
society and culture has developed and fostered. Moreover,
they all tend to be attracted to some form of authentic socialism
that would allow everyone to attain complete fulfillment as
human beings. They are opposed to the official religion of the
prevailing system because they view it as an empty formula or a
force fostering alienation. Yet many of them retain an essentially religious attitude; or at least they are trying to find and
live some sort of authentic fellowship and love, which is the
foundation of all valid religion.

This new awareness of liberation and the resultant search
for it range from the pacifist utopias of hippies in the world of
consumerism to the guerrilla movements that are to be found
mainly in the world of enforced silence. It is particularly evident in the explosive concern for liberation among certain
groups of Christians who have taken on new life.

There is no doubt that the hippies played an important role
in this new awareness of inhumanism in the capitalistic world.
Children of that culture, they personally experienced the suffocating atmosphere of a depersonalized, empty world that
seemed familiar only with objects, numbers, timetables, and
frozen routines. Their rejection of that culture was to be a
complete and radical one. Aware of the limitations of violence
and pessimistic over the chances of changing the world, they
chose to flee from it as the medieval monks had done. They
gathered together in rural communities of a socialist cast or in
communal apartments in the big cities. They wanted to live a
tranquil life based on peace, love, and brotherhood—a better
life than the one promised by their society, its power structure,
its formulas, its religion, and its God.

Because they wanted complete sincerity and authenticity,
their rejection of the existing world had to be definitive and

absolute. It had to include the image of God proffered by their society, for that God allowed people to act hypocritically, to sanctify egotism, oppression, discrimination, war, and murder. Religion was a surface mask, a mere by-product of societal life without any real depth or impact on practice. Yearning for freedom and a truly human life, they rebelled against the falseness and mannerism of the culture and the reifying impact of its emphasis on "having." They agreed with what Harvey Cox had to say in *The Feast of Fools*. Society had turned life and religion into something far too serious and somber. It was time to get back to the spirit of festivity in all its forms. It was time to learn how to enjoy small joys and to delight over life and love.

It is quite obvious that this youth protest, which was so much in vogue only a few years ago, was essentially religious and subversive, though it claimed to do without God. Those young people were looking for a different world, a world based on community. Their quest found expression in the liturgy of their rock music and in their week-long music festivals, in their attempts to find nirvana through drugs and psychedelic experiences, in their practice of love toward all, and even in the austerity of their shared living and their detachment from all the superfluous goods of a consumerist world.

Today the hippies are fading out of the picture. Their own excesses combined with the system's commercialization of them to rob their movement of its essential note of protest. But though hippies may be on the decline, the genuine uneasiness that gave rise to them in the first place is not. This uneasiness is essentially religious in nature—in the biblical and prophetic sense of that term. For it looks toward the creation of a world where real communication between one human being and another, and between human beings and God, will be possible once again. It is this uneasiness and anxious searching that underlies the new "Jesus movement" and all the various groups—Jesus freaks, Pentecostals—who are tending to move apart from the official church and to advocate a new style of community life. They all want a life of love that is closer to the lineaments of Jesus' own gospel.[14]

Besides these movements that usually are of a pacifist cast, and besides the various brands of atheistic humanism of which I shall speak in Part III, I must also mention the various revolutionary movements that advocate the construction of a better world on the ruins of the present order as well as the new socialist consciousness that is now gaining ground steadily. We are witnessing the rise of new versions of Marxism and Christianity. They are antidogma and antisystem open to dialogue and joint action, humanistic and fleshed out in the concrete reality of the world of oppression. These new versions of Marxism and Christianity are the chief motivating force behind the uneasy quest for a new world. In Latin America, for example, it is encouraging to note that more and more Christian groups are becoming aware of the political dimension of the faith and how it can be incarnated in fraternal liberation praxis.

In the past the term "revolutionary" was almost synonymous with the term "atheist." Today we are beginning to realize that the best synonym for "revolutionary" is not "atheist" but "Christian." It is this new way of living the Christian faith and engaging in theological reflection that I shall consider in Part II.

Notes

1. See G. Vahanian, "Theology and the End of the Age of Religion," in *Concilium* 25 (New York: Paulist Press, 1967).

2. Mircea Eliade, *The Sacred and the Profane: The Nature of Religion* (New York: Harper Torchbooks, 1961), pp. 207 and 213.

3. See Etienne Gilson, "The Idea of God and the Difficulties of Atheism," in *The Great Ideas Today* (Chicago: Encyclopaedia Britannica, 1969), pp. 239–74, especially pp. 251–52.

4. "No empirical scientists can manage to prove the existence of God; the proofs proposed by physicists and biologists tend only to falsify the idea of God" (R. Jolivet, *Le Dieu des philosophes et des savants* [Paris, 1956], pp. 75–78; Eng. trans.: *The God of Reason* [New York: Hawthorn, 1958]).

5. Karl Rahner puts it this way: "God is not a part of the world but its pre-requisite; he is not an objective piece of knowledge alongside other objects, but the endlessness always already present prior to the movement of knowledge, the endlessness within which it runs its always finite course. God is not the final hypothesis resulting from a sketching-in of a rounded picture of the world, he is on the contrary the single thesis which is posited with every hypothesis which we use to build up our picture of the world. . . . Today . . . the world has become a quantity rounded in itself, which is not really open at various points where it makes a transition to God, which does not suffer at determinate points observable by us the causal impact of God on it . . . but only as a whole and very undemonstratively does it point up to God as its precondition. . . . God is inexpressively elevated above everything that is or can be thought outside himself. . . . That this is so is realized by mankind today, since it has come gradually into possession of a scientific picture of the world which is as profane as the world which is not God. . . . We are just discovering today that one cannot picture God to oneself in an image that has been carved out of the wood of the world. The academic of today has the duty, which is at once pain and grace, of accepting this realization, of not suppressing it in a hasty and cheap apologetics for an anthropomorphic 'belief in God,' of interpreting it rightly, that is, of understanding that it has in truth nothing to do with atheism in the proper sense" ("Science as a 'Confession'?" *Theological Investigations*, Eng. trans. [Baltimore: Helicon, 1967], 3:388–91).

6. See E. Borne, *Sources et cheminements de l'athéisme* (Paris: Ed. du Cerf, 1963), p. 111.

7. See De Finance: "There is no longer any recourse to religious transcendence. Or, to be more precise, there is no longer any feeling that we need to have such recourse insofar as we hide from ourselves and repress part of ourselves, insofar as we refuse to accept the innermost urgings of our being and our reality. The truly human mark of such a reality would be the fact that we raised questions about our own destiny. But religious language is no longer given any credit within the technological world. There is no longer any place for religious categories in a world where people have claimed to wipe out any and all analogical signs of the divine, in a world where everything is written

down in pragmatic terms, in terms of our ability to produce and consume" (De Finance et al., *Psicología del ateísmo* [Madrid: Ed. Paulinas, 1968], p. 22).

8. With this in mind, Berdyaev asked himself whether the creatures who would inherit the modern world truly deserved to be called human beings at all since they either denied or were ignorant of their capabilities that were most truly human. Eugene Fontinelli is thinking along the same lines when he suggests that today's people of reason may not really be "reasonable" human beings. The "people of reason" are locked up in the results arrived at by their own brains. Truly reasonable human beings, while recognizing the importance of reason and never acting in direct contradiction to its findings, would also recognize other cognitive dimensions that are equally human. Acknowledging that reason cannot solve the question of God's existence on its own, truly reasonable people will admit that human beings must live in accordance with principles that transcend reason (See Eugene Fontinelli, "Reflections on Faith and Metaphysics," in Denis Dirscherl, ed., *Speaking of God* [Milwaukee: Bruce, 1967], p. 119).

9. "Modern civilization permits the sights of death in a sensationalist, chilling aspect. . . . Press photographers, who are well paid for their work, must hunt out death to satisfy this demand. People shroud the reality of death in a veil of silence, either making it banal or denying it completely" (Dieter Oberndöfer, *La soledad del hombre en la sociedad norteamericana,* Spanish edition [Madrid: Ed. Rialp, 1964]).

10. "Alfred Kinsey," cover story in *Time,* August 24, 1953, p. 58.

11. David Riesman, *The Lonely Crowd* (New Haven: Yale University Press, paperback edition, 1961), pp. 146–47.

12. In his *Economic and Philosophic Manuscripts,* Marx presented a masterful description of the deifying character of money. Commenting on Shakespeare's *Timon of Athens,* he writes: "My power, like the power of money, is great. The properties of money are my properties as its possessor. Thus *what I am* and *what I can do* are not determined in the least by my own individuality. I may be ugly, but I can buy myself the most beautiful woman. Hence I am not really ugly because the effect of ugliness . . . has been eliminated by money. As an individual, I may be a cripple. But with money I can buy myself twenty-four good legs; hence I am not a cripple at all. I may be a dishonest and dishonorable man . . . but since money is honored, its possessor will also be honored. Money is the supreme good, so its possessor is also good."

13. E. Fromm, *The Art of Loving* (New York: Bantam paperback edition, 1970), p. 73.

14. The success of *Godspell* and *Jesus Christ Superstar,* along with the widespread diffusion of buttons, posters, and ads featuring Jesus, is a clear indication that the person and lifestyle of Jesus is highly attractive to many young people today.

PART II

GOD AND HUMAN LIBERATION

5

GOD: OUR LIBERATOR

Thus the Lord saved Israel on that day from the power of the Egyptians. When Israel saw the Egyptians lying dead on the seashore and beheld the great power that the Lord had shown against the Egyptians, they feared the Lord and believed in him and in his servant Moses.

Exod. 14:30–31

God has indeed spoken, and he has spoken about himself. So rather than trying to work up some image or some new concept of God for ourselves, we must listen to his own word and accept it. I fully realize that in writing these words I am stepping out of the confines of philosophy and plunging into the obscure regions of faith. I do so because it is my conscious belief that we must make that choice if we really want to say something valid about God. We human beings cannot comprehend God, we can only listen to what God has to say to us. The God of science and scholarship will ever remain an idol. Even the best efforts of philosophy can do nothing more than point up the need for an Absolute Being as the foundation of all that exists. Before the God of philosophy we cannot bend our knees or pray or love, as Heidegger has pointed out. Such a God ever remains a mere concept, an idol. He is not and never can be the liberator God whom the Bible presents to us.

I want to make it quite clear that in the following pages I shall be speaking to you as a Christian, as a human being who truly believes that God did manifest himself to us in the series of saving events that are presented in the literature of the Bible. I truly believe that he manifested himself in a special way in Jesus, so that God's presence was embodied in a human being.

To this word or message of God, my response is the "yes" of faith. It is not the mere intellectual acceptance of certain ideas or precepts. It is a concrete praxis framed in the context of God's plan to humanize the world and to convert humanity into the brotherhood inspired by love. I interpret faith in God to be a transforming praxis and a gift of love toward one's fellows, not simply a matter of intellectual acceptance or a yearning for security and certainty. That is how I understand the word of God presented to us by the Christian message. That is how I understand the human response which it inspires and calls for. In my opinion that word and that response provide the best answer for the question that ever lies before us: What exactly is the world and humanity?

We human beings have rejected God, judging his image was an attack on our freedom and grandeur. We have conjured up utopias both in heaven and on earth. Without any longer feeling a trace of anxiety, we accept the absence of the silent lodger who has accompanied us from the very start. But in the cold void left by the absence of God, we are now beginning to feel the wound of our radical finiteness and contingency even as we sense the dehumanizing character of a world that sought to be fully human by eliminating God.

The word of God remains ever committed to the cause of man's liberation. Once upon a time man dreamed that he could be fully free and human only by rejecting God. Today he is beginning to realize that only God can really make him free, that only God can guarantee his humanness. Why? Because God wants freedom for man even more than man himself does.

Creation

No message comes across clearer in the Bible than the fact that God is the liberator of human beings. Time and again in the Bible we see people rejecting their covenant relationship and community and heading back down the road of oppression and dehumanization. Time and again in the Bible we see God making every effort to ensure that people will live in freedom and kinship.

The message of creation is clear. God created us in his own image. We were fashioned for a community based on love: "God created man in his image, in the divine image he created him; male and female he created them. God blessed them, saying, 'Be fertile and multiply, fill the earth and subdue it' " (Gen. 1:27–28). God, a community of love, chose to create us in his image. We, too, are to be a community of love; and we are given dominion over the earth to rule and transform it (Gen. 1:26–30).

So God did not place humanity in a finished, perfect world. He created us to be transforming agents, doers, subjects; and he invited us to fulfill his vocation of love in the work of transforming the world and making it more human. We appear in the onrushing flow of a process that cannot be stopped. We appear on the face of an earth already filled with plants and animals, where the prevailing law seems to be the survival of the strongest. God establishes us in that world and gives us the task of transforming it and making it ever more human. In and through the power of love we are to fashion a perfect community. We must never forget that we are the master of the plants and animals, that we are not to submit to creatures lower than ourselves. Only Yahweh, our creator, is our God. Only God is worthy of our adoration. Animals, plants, the objects of nature and of our own handicraft are mere creatures designed to serve us.

Thus the message of creation is tremendously positive. Humankind, as male and female, is meant to be a community of love. This community is loved by God in turn, and it is established here on earth to transform and humanize the world so that it will be a fitting place for the communal life of love. We are the rulers of the world, of a world that is good and that must be cared for scrupulously. We must love the world rather than subjecting it to indiscriminate destruction.[1]

Almost at once the Bible sets the history of human sinfulness alongside God's plan of love. Human beings quickly attempt to fashion their own happiness in their own way. Adam sins, attempting to be like God and to know "what is good and what is bad" (Gen. 3:5). In trying to strike out on a new road of his own, he destroys his communal life of love. The history of sin sets people against each other. Adam turns against Eve (Gen. 3:12), Cain turns against Abel (Gen. 4:1–15), and the earth is filled with "lawlessness" (Gen. 6:13). Human beings sow egotism in their hearts, substituting the rule of force for the community of love and thereby returning to the realm of animality and force. They tell God that they will fashion their own city in their own way, and they go so far as to build a Babel against God's wishes. But when human beings choose to live without God, they also turn against each other. Babel symbolizes the definitive rupture of community life; human beings can no longer understand each other and all set off in their own directions. (Gen. 11:1–9). Egotism replaces love and violence reigns. We could find no better interpretation or psychological description of the present-day world.

Yet God does not abandon us. The more we attempt to cut out our own path based on alienation and oppression, the more God pursues us and invites us to get back on his path toward true freedom and liberation. The history of human infidelity is paralleled by the history of a patient God and his covenant. God keeps hoping in human beings, keeps trying to make us free despite what we ourselves do to the contrary.

The Exodus

The Exodus is the touchstone and foundation of all biblical thinking about God. In a series of concrete salvific events, Israel is freed from bondage in Egypt. It is an act of liberation on the international level. Israel's faith in Yahweh is rooted in that series of events and constantly draws nourishment from it. Its whole history is organized around that saving action. When later writers talk about Yahweh, they constantly go back to the image of Yahweh as the liberator, the one who led Israel out of bondage in Egypt.

The Exodus is a perfect description of the slow and arduous process whereby a people attains its liberation. God chooses one people to whom he will reveal himself in a special way. It is an enslaved and oppressed people (Exod. 1:11–14), a people savagely mistreated by the Egyptians (Exod. 2:11). God sees the suffering and oppression of this people. He commits himself to the task of liberating them, and in the process he will reveal himself to them. He does not reveal himself as a static, immobile God but as an active doer. He is the God who effects the liberation of oppressed human beings.

The decision of pharaoh and his armies is an oppressive one that denies the work of humanization. Yahweh reacts against that decision, choosing to create a nation of free human beings and to reactivate his plan for a loving community through those who are being exploited in this world. The journey toward liberation will be long and tortuous, filled with ups and downs. There will be illusions, temptations to give up and turn back. But standing above those vicissitudes and giving direction to the process is Yahweh's irrevocable decision to make people free.

The process of liberation begins with an act of violence. Moses, upset by the oppression endured by his people and by the cruelty of their Egyptian overlords, kills an Egyptian (Exod. 2:12). Right from the start, then, the Exodus speaks out against the pusillanimity and hypocrisy of a world that condemns violence even as it instigates it. It makes it clear to us that violence can be just and necessary if it is truly liberative.

Then comes Moses' own doubt and his temptation to desert the cause. He will let things remain as they are because liberation seems impossible in any case. He feels incapable of carrying out the mission and so he asks God to send someone else in his place (Exod. 4:13). Though he complains of his own lack of eloquence (Exod. 4:10; 6:12; 6:30) and Yahweh acknowledges his frailty (Exod. 3:11), Yahweh himself will not retreat from his plan to free his people. He issues a command to Moses and assures him: "I will be with you" (Exod. 3:12).

Moses takes heart and sets out on his mission. His word begins to instill hope in the Israelites; they begin to look forward to the day of their liberation. Faced with this situation, the Egyptians intensify their oppression. The oppressed Israelites begin to lose heart once again and even to turn against their would-be liberators: "The Lord look upon you and judge! You have brought us into bad odor with pharaoh and his servants and have put a sword in their hands to slay us" (Exod. 5:21).

Despite the vacillation and backsliding of his people, God will see to it that they do escape from bondage despite all the obstacles posed by their oppressors. It is a long and violent struggle. The firstborn of the Egyptians die, and there is loud wailing throughout Egypt (Exod. 12:29–30). Yahweh's decision eventually prevails when waters flow in to drown "the chariots and charioteers of pharaoh's whole army" (Exod. 14:27–28). Realizing that they have just experienced the presence and power of their God, the Israelites burst into a joyous hymn of thanksgiving:

I will sing to the Lord, for he is gloriously triumphant; horses and chariots he has cast into the sea. My strength and my courage is the Lord, and he has been my savior. He is my God, I praise him; the God of my father, I extol him. The Lord is a warrior, Lord is his name! Pharaoh's chariots and army he hurled into the sea; the elite of his officers were submerged in the Red Sea. The flood waters covered them, they sank into the depths like a stone. Your right hand, O Lord, magnificent in power, your right hand, O Lord, has shattered the enemy. In your great majesty you overthrew your adversaries; you loosed your wrath to consume them like stubble. At a breath of your anger the waters piled up, the flowing waters stood like a mound, the flood waters congealed in the midst of the sea. The enemy boasted, "I will pursue and overtake them; I will divide the spoils and have my fill of them; I will draw my sword; my hand shall despoil them!" When your wind blew, the sea covered them; like lead they sank in the mighty waters. Who is like to you among the gods, O Lord? Who is like to you, magnificent in holiness? O terrible in renown, worker of wonders, when you stretched out your right hand, the earth swallowed them! In your mercy you led the people you redeemed; in your strength you guided them to your holy dwelling. The nations heard and quaked; anguish gripped the dwellers in Philistia. Then were the princes of Edom dismayed; trembling seized the chieftains of Moab; all the dwellers in Canaan melted away; terror and dread fell upon them. By the might of your arm they were frozen like stone, while your people, O Lord, passed over, while the people you had made your own passed over. And you brought them in and planted them on the mountain of your inheritance—the place where you made your seat, O Lord, the sanctuary, O Lord, which your hands established. The Lord shall reign forever and ever [Exod. 15:1–18].

This first victory was not the end of the story, however. The people liberated from the house of bondage would have to endure a long journey filled with hardship, want, and inimical attacks before they could settle down in community. Once again they gave way to delusions and began to long for Egypt: "Here in the desert the whole Israelite community grumbled against Moses and Aaron. The Israelites said to them, 'Would that we had died at the Lord's hand in the land of Egypt, as we sat by our fleshpots and ate our fill of bread! But you had to lead us into this desert to make the whole community die of famine!' " (Exod. 16:2–3).[2] Once again Yahweh did not abandon them. Heeding their cries, he provided them with food "so that you may know that I, the Lord, am your God (Exod. 16:12). They were to share this food as a community, so that all would have enough (Exod. 16:18).

Having liberated his people, God laid down his law of brotherhood in his decalogue. Right at the start it sets forth the true basis of such brotherhood: "You shall not have other gods besides me" (Exod. 20:3). Only Yahweh the liberator can be the God of human beings. Going back to other gods and worshipping the works of one's own hand means turning back to the path of bondage and slavery. Only the liberator God can guarantee communion between human beings. The rest of the commandments in the decalogue shore up the life of the community. "They prohibit all enslavement to egotism, hatred, avarice, jealousy, and sexuality. It is possible to serve God only by living as brothers. This stands in direct contrast to a society ruled by the principle of selfish individual interests. It is poles apart from our present-day capitalistic world."[3] Indeed the whole spirit of the decalogue and the other precepts in the book of Deuteronomy is summed up in a pithy command of major importance that we find in the book of Leviticus. It lays down the basis for all authentic community life: "You shall treat the alien who resides with you no differently than the natives born among you; have the same love for him as for yourself" (Lev. 19:34).

Once again, however, the Hebrews are disloyal to Yahweh and forget their promises of fidelity. They fashion a golden calf to worship, finding it too difficult to worship a God whom they cannot see and who demands so much of them. Growing weary of the struggle for liberation, they decide to worship the idol fashioned by their own hands. The idol makes no demands on them, and they can worship it with a feeling of security (Exod. 32). They are weary of privations: "We remember the fish we used to eat without cost in Egypt, and the cucumbers, the melons, the leeks, the onions, and the garlic" (Num. 11:5). Words of protest arise once again: "Why did you lead us out of Egypt, only to bring us to this wretched place which has neither grains nor figs nor vines nor pomegranates? Here there is not even water to drink!" (Num. 20:5). They are in a rebellious mood and begin to talk about returning to Egypt: "So they said to one another, 'Let us appoint a leader and go back to Egypt' " (Num. 14:4).

The journey to liberation is long and arduous. We grow weary of the trip and begin to think nostalgically of our old state of bondage. Austerity and freedom do not seem half so attractive as relative affluence and bondage. Yet it is God's decision to make us free, and that decision will prevail. After a long and arduous exodus, Yahweh bequeathes the promised land to the Hebrews. In that history we find a living and concrete example of the history of all authentic liberation. It is suffused with the active presence of God, who desires and works for liberation even more than we ourselves do.

The Prophets

As time went by, the Israelites forgot the communitarian laws that God had laid down and they had accepted.[4] Oppression and injustice took root in Israel, and the people merrily indulged in infidelity to Yahweh. Shutting their eyes to the practices of a futile and insincere religion, they forgot that Yahweh wanted them to practice justice and brotherhood. They hoped to blind God in a cloud of sacrifice and incense. Instead of expressing relationships based on justice, religion was used to camouflage and compensate for an inhuman life-style. It ceased to serve as the leaven for a truly fraternal society, to perform its denunciatory role. It became an opiate, impeding the work of fellowship.

It was then that Yahweh sent his prophets to remind his people of the real meaning of authentic religion. The Israelites must perform works of justice and practice fidelity to Yahweh. Of the people, the prophets are pillars in the history of libera-tion. Curt and forceful, their voices toppled the false struc-tures of the nations, shaking up people who had turned the task of liberation into a mere memory.

Discarnate sacrifices and prayers are not what Yahweh wants from his people. Amos, Hosea, Isaiah, Jeremiah, and Micah make it clear that Yahweh wants justice and fraternal relations. Any religion based on unjust social relationships is a false religion:

I hate, I spurn your feasts. I take no pleasure in your solemnities. Your cereal offerings I will not accept, nor consider your stall-fed peace offerings. . . . But if you would offer me holocausts, then let justice surge like water, and goodness like an unfailing stream [Amos 5:21–24].

What care I for the number of your sacrifices? says the Lord. I have had enough of whole-burnt rams and fat of fatlings; in the blood of calves, lambs and goats I find no pleasure. When you come in to visit me, who asks these things of you? Trample my courts no more! Bring no more worthless offerings; your incense is loathsome to me. New moon and sabbath, calling of assemblies, octaves with wickedness: these I cannot bear. . . . When you spread out your hands, I close my eyes to you; though you pray the more, I will not listen. Your hands are full of blood! Wash yourselves clean! Put away your misdeeds from before my eyes. Cease to do evil, learn to do good. Make justice your aim: redress the wronged, hear the orphan's plea, defend the widow [Isa. 1:11–18].

"Why do we fast, and you do not see it? afflict ourselves, and you take no note of it?" Lo, on your fast day you carry out your own pursuits, and drive all your laborers. Yes, your fast ends in quarreling and fighting, striking with wicked claw. Would that today you might fast so as to make your voice heard on high! Is this the manner of fasting I wish, of keeping a day of penance: That a man bow his head like a reed, and lie in sackcloth and ashes? Do you call this a fast, a day acceptable to the Lord? This, rather, is the fasting that I wish: releasing those bound unjustly, untying the thongs of the yoke, setting free the oppressed, breaking every yoke, sharing your bread with the hungry, sheltering the oppressed and the homeless, clothing the naked when you see them, and not turning your back on your own. Then your light shall break forth like the dawn, and your wound shall quickly be healed. Your vindication shall go before you, and the glory of the Lord shall be your rear guard. Then you shall call, and the Lord will answer. You shall cry for help and he will say: Here I am! If you remove from your midst oppression, false accusation and malicious speech, if you bestow your bread on the hungry and satisfy the afflicted, then light shall rise for you in the darkness and the gloom shall become for you like midday [Isa. 58:3–10].

The primary role and task of religion is the establishment of a world based on just relationships. To overlook that fact is to prostitute religion. By the same token, every commitment to a more humane world and to the eradication of oppression is "anonymously" religious. It is after the heart of all true religion.[5] According to the prophets, faith in God must be converted into the concrete praxis of liberation. It has political, economic, and social dimensions. To believe in God is to work for justice and to serve those in need. To be authentic, religion must be fleshed out in the struggle for a more humane world. God is on the side of people and their liberation, fighting against structures that continue to oppress them. To accept God is to opt for liberation and to take a stand on the side of the people.[6]

A world in which religion has lost all socio-political embodiment is a world turned false; it is doomed to destruction. The message of the prophets is a violent and tragic message. It is a revolutionary message against oppressive structures. Amos, Hosea, Isaiah, Jeremiah, Micah, Zephaniah, and Malachi announce that Yahweh will punish his people for the abuses they have committed, for their failure to act in accordance with justice. The "day of Yahweh" will be one of catastrophic punishment. Yahweh will reveal his power to his people, but in a terrible way:

Therefore, because of you, Zion shall be plowed like a field, and Jerusalem reduced to rubble, and the mount of the temple to a forest ridge [Mic. 3:12].

For the Lord of hosts will have his day against all that is proud and arrogant, all that is high, and it will be brought low. Yes, against all the cedars of Lebanon and all the oaks of Bashan, against all the lofty mountains and all the high hills, against every lofty tower and every fortified wall, against all the ships of Tarshish and all stately vessels. Human pride will be abased, the arrogance of men brought low, and the Lord alone will be exalted on that day [Isa. 2:12–17].

At that time I will explore Jerusalem with lamps. I will punish the men who thicken on their lees, who say in their hearts, "Neither good nor evil can the Lord do." Their wealth shall be given to pillage, and their houses to devastation. They will build houses but shall not dwell in them, plant vineyards but not drink their wine. Near is the great day of the Lord, near and very swiftly coming. Hark, the day of the Lord! Bitter, then, the warrior's cry. A day of wrath is that day, a day of anguish and distress, a day of destruction and desolation, a day of darkness and gloom, a day of thick black clouds, a day of trumpet blasts and battle alarm against fortified cities, against battlements on high. I will hem men in till they walk like the blind, because they have sinned against the Lord; and their blood shall be poured out like dust, and their brains like dung. Neither their silver nor their gold shall be able to save them on the day of the Lord's wrath, when in the fire of his jealousy all the earth shall be consumed. For he shall make an end, yes, a sudden end, of all who live on the earth [Zeph. 1:12–18].

For lo, the day is coming, blazing like an oven, when all the proud and all evildoers will be stubble. And the day that is coming will set them on fire, leaving them neither root nor branch, says the Lord of hosts [Mal. 3:19].

But God has not forgotten his will to liberate people. He continues to work for that goal even though they choose to be slaves time and again. The Lord comforts his people and shows mercy to his afflicted (Isa. 49:13). Even though a mother might forget her child, Yahweh will not forget Israel (Isa. 49:15–16). Liberation will surge up anew from the ruins of an unjust world, just as real kinship will rise from the ashes of the earlier relationships marked by inhumanity. There will be "new" human beings with a very different sort of heart: "I will give them a new heart and put a new spirit within them. I will remove the stony heart from their bodies and replace it with a natural heart, so that they will live according to my statutes, and observe and carry out my ordinances" (Ezek. 11:19–20).

These new human beings will live lives based on love rather than on injustice, and God himself will effect this liberation. In the turmoil of its history Israel begins to glimpse the hope of a liberating Messiah:

He shall rescue the poor man when he cries out, and the afflicted when he has no one to help him. He shall have pity for the lowly and the poor; the lives of the poor he shall save. From fraud and violence he shall redeem them, and precious shall their blood be in his sight [Ps. 72:12–14].

Here is my servant whom I uphold, my chosen one with whom I am pleased, upon whom I have put my spirit. He shall bring forth justice to the nations, not crying out, not shouting, not making his voice heard in the street. A bruised reed he shall not break, and a smoldering wick he shall not quench, until he establishes justice on the earth. The coastlands will wait for his teaching. Thus says God, the Lord, who created the heavens and stretched them out, who spreads out the earth with its crops, who gives breath to its people and spirit to those who walk on it: I, the Lord, have called you for the victory of justice. I have grasped you by the hand. I formed you and set you as a covenant of the people, a light for the nations, to open the eyes of the blind, to bring out prisoners from confinement, and from the dungeon those who live in darkness [Isa. 42:1–7; cf. 61:1–2].

Jesus

So when the "fullness of time" arrived, Jesus came. God's commitment to human liberation led him to take on flesh and blood, to become a living embodiment of the concrete way to liberation. That is precisely what Jesus was and is: God's way of liberating us.

Jesus appears to be just another human being. He is a man of the people, a child of the laboring class that inhabits the towns and villages of Israel. He was born in one of the most insignificant towns of Palestine, in the midst of a phony peace that was maintained by the armed force of Rome's legions. Once again God's liberation is fleshed out in an oppressed people, in a common figure of whom no one takes any notice (Isa. 53:2–3). God's message of liberation is astonishingly clear and consistent: Liberation will not come from the top, from the intellectuals and politicians who play games with the common people; it will come from below, from those who are suffering from oppression. God is on the side of those who suffer from injustice; God is in their very midst.

God's message for us is epitomized in the figure of Jesus. Purified of all shortcomings, it is fleshed out in him. Jesus did not come to suppress or destroy the earlier teachings of Moses and the prophets; he came to fulfill them completely and perfectly (Matt. 5:17). A note of urgency characterizes his mission and his message, for the time of definitive liberation is close at hand: "This is the time of fulfillment. The reign of God is at hand! Reform your lives and believe in the gospel!" His message draws the proletariat of Palestine, kindling their dreams of an earthly kingdom marked by affluence. They see Jesus as their liberator, as the Messiah who had been foretold long ago and who would redeem them from bondage and misery. Indeed Jesus does present himself to them in that light.[7] One day he enters the synagogue in Nazareth and reads the prophetic words of Isaiah:

He unrolled the scroll and found the passage where it was written, "The spirit of the Lord is upon me; therefore he has anointed me. He has sent me to bring glad tidings to the poor, to proclaim liberty to captives, recovery of sight to the blind and release to prisoners, to announce a year of favor from the Lord." Rolling up the scroll he gave it back to the assistant and sat down. All in the synagogue had their eyes fixed on him. Then he began by saying to them, "Today this Scripture passage is fulfilled in your hearing" [Luke 4:17–21].

Thus Jesus presents himself as the liberator of the oppressed. Immersed in the very heart of oppressive structures, he proclaims a new world, a kingdom of justice and kinship. He is the Messiah of this new liberty, the presence of God among us. God is still at work on the task of fashioning a world of free people, and he is fleshed out in Jesus. Israel had been dreaming of a political Messiah, of a great king who would lead it to conquest and victory. The Jews were hoping to break the chains of oppression and do some oppressing themselves. They had not yet gotten over their own will to exercise power in an oppressive way. Jesus' message goes right to the heart of the problem, attacking the egotism rooted deeply in their hearts.

Jesus makes it clear that it will not do simply to overthrow the Roman oppressors and then take their place. Human beings must lay the groundwork for a new world where there are neither oppressors nor oppressed, neither slaves nor masters, neither rich nor poor. It is a radical and thorough kinship that is to serve as the foundation of this new world order or kingdom. Jesus' essential message, the new commandment he gives his disciples, is a summons to love. Love is the quality that will serve as the distinguishing feature of his followers (John 13:34; 15:12, 17).

By its very nature love is a dynamic and active force. It goes out of itself and tries to create community. It does not tolerate injustice and inequality. It liberates people from everything that stands in the way of communion. It sees all human beings as active subjects and brothers and sisters. It rejects all abuse or exploitation. That is why it cannot help but seem to be a subversive force in a world characterized by oppression and injustice. If it is to destroy injustice and oppression, if it is to clear the way for true communion, it must have force and bite of its own.

This explains why there will be no room for certain people in the kingdom of Jesus: the rich, whose hearts are given over to their own possessions; those in power, who use power to oppress other human beings; those who are consumed with pride and arrogance; those who cheat the poor; those who do not love. The concrete practice of love will be the standard by which humanity is judged on the decisive day at the end of time. The Son of Man will condemn those who had closed their hearts to their needy fellows, to the people with whom Jesus identified himself. Those who had lived a life of service will be rewarded, even though they may not have realized that they were serving Jesus when they served their needy fellows. The judgment scene will be a great surprise to many:

When the Son of Man comes in his glory, escorted by all the angels of heaven, he will sit upon his royal throne, and all the nations will be assembled before him. Then he will separate them into two groups, as a shepherd separates sheep from goats. The sheep he will place on his right hand, the goats on his left. The king will say to those on his right: "Come. You have my Father's blessing! Inherit the kingdom prepared for you from the creation of the world. For I was hungry and you gave me food, I was thirsty and you gave me drink. I was a stranger and you welcomed me, naked and you clothed me. I was ill and you comforted me, in prison and you came to visit me." Then the just will ask him: "Lord, when did we see you hungry and feed you, or see you thirsty and give you drink? When did we welcome you away from home or clothe you in your nakedness? When did we visit you when you were ill or in prison?" The king will answer them: "I assure you, as often as you did it for one of my least brothers, you did it for me."

Then he will say to those on his left: "Out of my sight, you condemned into that everlasting fire prepared for the devil and his angels! I was hungry and you gave me no food, I was thirsty and you gave me no drink. I was away from home and you gave me no welcome, naked and you gave me no clothing. I was ill and in prison and you did not come to comfort me." Then they in turn will ask: "Lord, when did we see you hungry or thirsty or away from home or naked or ill or in prison and not attend you in your needs?" He will answer them: "I assure you, as often as you neglected to do it to one of these least ones, you neglected to do it to me" [Matt. 25:31–46].

Following directly in the footsteps of the prophets, Jesus asserts that authentic faith and religion must be converted into practice, a practice designed to liberate one's fellow human beings. Believing in God means serving the needy, helping the wounded wayfarer on the road, and fashioning the kingdom in the midst of human beings. While the gospel message is not a compendium of revolutionary strategy or a treatise on the organization of economics and social life, it obviously conveys and propagates the spirit that must come before any tactical or organizational work. Those who practice love and stand on the side of justice are also on Jesus' side. Those who maintain loveless structures and opt for injustice are against him.

The love that Jesus demands of his followers also takes in their enemies. There is no place for vengeance in the new society that Jesus wants. We are not to oppress those who had been our oppressors. We are not to follow the loveless standards that they had followed. Loving one's oppressors means liberating them from their status as oppressors. We must combat them if that is necessary to stop their work of oppression. We must accept them as our brothers and sisters once they have recovered their humanness. And this love for human liberation and the eradication of injustice may entail dying for the sake of others, as it did in Jesus' own case (1 John 13:16).

It is only natural that Jesus' message of love would seem rebellious and subversive to those who maintain and support the existing structures of oppression. Those who choose to love as Jesus did in his life must be prepared to face the same fate, and we know what that fate was. Rome and Israel, the prevailing political and religious interests in the contemporary system, joined forces to kill him. His love was just too dangerous. They brought him to trial and found him deserving of the death penalty. They erected a cross for him, and this rebel advocating liberty died amid the scorns and jeers of people who had been manipulated by the great ones of the world.

His cry of abandonment on Good Friday, however, was actually the death-knell of all the powers of oppression. Here we come to one of the essential points in the gospel's message of liberation. Christ was made sin, as Paul puts it. In his own flesh, all the forces of sin and the powers of lovelessness were crucified. But Good Friday was followed by Easter Sunday, apparent defeat by supreme victory, the cry of agony by the shout of victory. Jesus died, but Jesus also rose from the dead. Death, the final and ultimate enemy, was also conquered. Goodness and love triumphed once and for all, defeating the forces that had apparently won out on Good Friday.

Thus the history of the Exodus was repeated once more. There is a new Passover that put an end to the power of egotism and oppression and opened the way for a new kind of life marked by liberation. Definitive victory remains with those who are suffering from injustice and fighting to overcome it. Easter Sunday signals the definitive victory of all those who are suffering and struggling for the construction of a more humane world, who are trying to flesh out relationships based on love in all spheres of life. However painful and sorrow-laden it may be, their self-sacrifice is creating a new world and proving to be victorious in the end.

We have just seen how God's plan for human liberation maintains its implacable course. With Jesus Christ it reached a climax that we could never have imagined. God did not just pass himself off as a liberator. He did not just crucify human egotism in his own flesh, thereby guaranteeing the ultimate victory of goodness. God went so far as to convert each and every human being into God himself. He became incarnate in Christ, and Christ identified himself with every human being, particularly with those who seem to be the most insignificant: children (Matt. 10:42; 18:5), poor people, prisoners, the naked (Matt. 25:35–36), the persecuted (Acts 9:4–5), the unnoticed (Luke 10:29–37), and so forth. So true is this that we cannot love God if we despise human beings (1 John 4:20). Indeed if we despise our fellows, we cannot possibly know God; we are really murderers (1 John 3:14–15).

Atheists have commonly rejected God because they think him to be the enemy of humankind and an obstacle to potential human grandeur. Their cry against God is meant to be a cry in favor of humanity. But in our atheistic world this cry against God is turning into a cry against humanity itself. For the fact is that no one is more committed to human liberation than God is. The dream of atheism to turn human beings into God has already been turned into a reality and a sure promise in Christ. For he is the presence of God among human beings, the presence of God fleshed out in each and every human being.

Our course is clear. Only by loving people can we love God. Only by struggling for the liberation of all human beings can we believe in God. When all is said and done, we must conclude that the biblical message is a dynamic, active, and liberative message. God is the enemy of false havens—of idols and golden calves and oppressive structures that block the road to liberation. The God of the Bible is opposed to any fixation with the status quo. He is opposed to those who would like to hold back the course of history, who would like to remain in bondage or go back to it.

The people of God is a people on exodus, a people following the footsteps of a God who invites them to journey toward their ultimate and definitive liberation. It is a lofty and demanding journey. Christians are asked to display the perfection of God himself in their relationships with their fellows: "You must be made perfect as your heavenly Father is perfect" (Matt. 5:48). Christians cannot hold back the course of revolution. They cannot rest content with partial victories in their revolutionary struggles. They must remain wayfarers throughout their lives, taking part in an ongoing process of revolution that will never end here. They must hunger and thirst for a better world. They must keep trying to root out oppression and to build a more humane world. They must remain steadfast in their opposition to everything that hinders the arrival of God's kingdom of love. They must keep hoping and fighting for the establishment of God's utopian kingdom here on earth.

The struggle is an arduous one, and it will always remain so; but Christians are assured of victory. They know that they are not alone on their journey. Their liberator God marches before them, and they can follow him confidently. The course is laden with idols that will try to detain them. But above all such lures they can hear the voice of their God urging them on, inviting them to build the kingdom of heaven on earth. Victory for them is certain because they have the word of him who said: "See, I make all things new!" (Rev. 21:5).

Notes

1. This point is taking on particular importance today because we are now experiencing the terrible consequences of a runaway technology. Nature is being contaminated and even destroyed. A theology of liberation must face up to this issue, of course, because the new humanity must be able to live with nature rather than destroying it. We must be liberated from our own destructive powers and tendencies before anything else.

2. See also Exod. 17:3: "Here, then, in their thirst for water, the people grumbled against Moses, saying, 'Why did you ever make us leave Egypt? Was it just to have us die here of thirst without children and our livestock?' "

3. José L. Caravias, *Vivir como hermanos* (Asunción: Loyola, 1971), p. 27.

4. See, for example, Num. 26:52–55; Deut. 19:14; 27:17.

5. Yahweh chooses and commissions Cyrus, a pagan who does not even know him, to rescue his people and take vengeance on their enemies. See Isa. 45.

6. See Caravias, *Vivir como hermanos*, p. 41.

7. Mark's whole Gospel presents Jesus' ministry as a liberation from Satan and his power, from the power of egotism in particular. Luke stresses that the first and foremost beneficiaries of Jesus' liberative work are the poor and oppressed. Paul presents Christ as the liberator of the Christian. Christ liberates us from the law and the trappings of the world (Gal. 2:16–17; 3:7–12; 5:6) so that we can live under the tutelage of love alone (Gal. 5:13–14). In his Epistle to the Romans, Paul provides a penetrating description of the world that retains all its relevance today. We want to move toward life but find ourselves slipping into the clutches of death. Sin proves to be victorious and we become dehumanized. But through his death Christ crucified sin and its consequences. His triumphant resurrection guarantees victory to Christians. Liberated by faith, Christians can live out their new-found liberty through works of service. John stresses that love is the norm of Christian life. It is a demanding practical love that must be embodied in deeds rather than in mere words. See Beltrán Villegas, "La liberación en la Biblia," *Teología y Vida* 13 (1972): 155–58.

6

TOWARD A NEW THEOLOGY

A new theology is arising which has not yet hit upon the idiom used in academic classrooms and convention halls. Indeed it might be wise for it to avoid that idiom altogether. This new theology has managed to cross the chasm that has stymied European theology, which has been trying to make itself understood by the discouraged and truly materialistic human beings of our technological culture. To do this, it has been forced to construct complicated conjectures in order to maintain God's right of citizenship in an atheistic world and to corroborate the resurrection in a world that has decisively broken off all communication with transcendence.

Latin American theology is now discovering that Christian faith is intrinsically *political. Adhering to Christ also entails establishing a relationship with the Father and having obligations to "others." It means entering a poor, oppressed family that cannot wait any longer, that urgently demands liberation.*

—Arturo Paoli

For all too many years Christian theology fostered uprootedness and apoliticism. Neglecting this earth, it concentrated one-sidedly on heaven. It taught the oppressed to be patient and resigned, and with its doctrine of original sin it even justified unjust situations and class differences. Even if only indirectly, then, it supported the selfish interests that maintained an oppressive world. Today, however, Christian theology is beginning to rediscover its earthly, political mission. Abandoning its ties to Greek and scholastic patterns of thought, it is beginning to take the road of the Bible and its prophets. It now looks toward confrontation and struggle, toward committed action and religion embodied in concrete works of justice, toward a divine promise that is both eschatological and earthy, toward faith as an incarnate praxis of liberation.

The Theology of Secularization

In my opinion, it was the theology of secularization that took the first steps toward bringing theology back down to earth. However timidly it moved in that direction, the theology of secularization did begin the work of bringing theology down from the rarefied atmosphere of heaven.

Dietrich Bonhoeffer, the pupil of Barth who was killed by the Nazis, was deeply concerned about the massive atheism of the modern world. He noted the serious discrepancy between religion and modern life. The starting point of his own theology was a strong stand against any form of pietism or religiosity. Religion, as he saw it, started with the assumption that people needed God to fulfill their desires and solve their problems. "Religious people speak of God when human perception is . . . at an end, or human resources fail. It is really always the *deus ex machina* they call to their aid, either for the so-called solving of insoluble problems or as support in human failure—always, that is to say, helping out human weakness or on the borders of human existence."[1]

Bonhoeffer pointed out that humankind was pushing those borders further and further back, that there were fewer and fewer connecting links between humankind (or nature) and God in our technological world. Thus "religious" faith would soon become totally irrelevant if it continued to stress our need for God in the old-fashioned sense and to operate with a metaphysics that people no longer took seriously. In the moral, political, and scientific fields God was no longer used as a working hypothesis. With our fund of knowledge and scientific accomplishments, we could now solve problems that we had once entrusted to God. So now we all must learn to live as if God did not exist at all. We must immerse ourselves in life and the world without relying on a God who is invoked to explain things or to fill the gaps in our knowledge and ability. God can no longer be used by us to evade the use of our freedom and our responsibilities toward others.

The world has come of age. It is senseless and ignoble to attack that adulthood, and it is also very unchristian. We cannot browbeat the world, urging it to return to its state of adolescence so that we can forcibly create a space for religion and God's action. The death-knell of "religion" has sounded. To be a Christian in the twentieth century is not to be religious but to be fully and completely human. Christians are beings for others, who drink the cup of earthly life to the last drop. They leave egotism aside and live their lives for other people. Authentic faith, the faith of human beings come of age, compels Christians to live secular lives and to fashion a more humane world through their religion: "God is teaching us that we must live as men who can get along very well without him. The God who is with us is the God who forsakes us (Mark 15:34). . . . Before God and with him we live without God. God allows himself to be edged out of the world and on to the cross. God is weak and powerless in the world, and that is exactly the way, the only way in which he can be with us and help us."[2]

Following Bonhoeffer's lead here, John Robinson raises a serious question in his book entitled *The New Reformation.*[3] He asks whether people living today shouldn't really be atheists. He suggests that there are three fundamental reasons that might indicate that people should indeed be atheists. First of all, God *is intellectually superfluous.* Modern science no longer needs God as a hypothesis in its theory or practice. By waiting for solutions from God, religion has in fact held up the course of scientific progress. Second, *God is emotionally unnecessary.* Human beings believe in themselves and each other. They do not need God for their emotional development and it is hard to find a place for him in the real difficulties they face. Third, *God is morally intolerable.* He causes human suffering and tragedy. Or, at the very least, he does not prevent such things even though he supposedly could.

Robinson does not succumb before these difficulties, however. He attempts to resolve them by analyzing Christian faith as a personal I-Thou relationship in the sense used by Martin Buber. Our faith, he says, should rule out any attempt to use God or to enter into a relationship of equality with him. Today more than ever before faith should be totally personal. It should be a relationship of love and trust in God for his own sake, not for any selfish or egotistical reasons. God is always a subject to be encountered in that way; he is never the explanation of some system or other. This new personal faith, however, need not be explicit. The atheist who lives a life of sincere commitment to some noble idea might very well be living an implicitly personal relationship with God in the I-Thou mold.

It was Robinson's *Honest to God,* which was published in 1963, that made him a household name and raised a storm in Christian circles. In that book Robinson called for a "Christian radicalism," a new vision of life and the world. Christians must be committed to the world and they must secularize the gospel message so that it can win over atheists. Christianity must be stripped of "mythology" as Bultmann suggests, of the "supernatural" as Tillich suggests, and of the "religious" as Bonhoeffer suggests. Robinson rejects a rigidly legalistic morality, recognizing the validity of some ethical relativism and stressing the priority of love in every ethical system. This love must be concrete and practical, seeing God in every neighbor.

These ideas about religion and secularization may well have been brought to the attention of the reading public more by Harvey Cox than by Bonhoeffer and Robinson. In *The Secular City* he offered a picture of the Christian city in our urban, technological, and secularized civilization. He suggested that in a certain sense religion was the "neurosis" of a culture whereas secularization was equivalent to maturity. The God of the Bible is the one who wants to move humanity toward maturity, and hence the community of faith must complete the task begun at creation and continued in the Exodus.

Secularization is taking cognizance of our duties and obligations toward this world and this life here. It is abandoning an alienating obsession with some world beyond or some here-after. Thanks to the progress of science, people now realize that the course of history is in their own hands. God has hidden himself from view in our world, but this hidden God is still somehow present. The outright "no" of the atheist to God is not correct.[4]

Cox maintains that it is biblical faith that is the root cause and justification for the present-day process of secularization. The concept and doctrine of creation clearly distinguished God from nature, stressing the distance between the two. It thus made it clear that only God is worthy of adoration and rever-ence. By denying that nature was in any way divine, the doc-trine of creation opened up the way for human questioning and transforming activity in the world. In a similar vein the Exodus desacralized politics. It broke with the sacred notion of kingship that prevailed in Egypt, thereby denying reverence and cultic worship to imperial or royal institutions. The Sinai covenant brought out the relativity of all human things by differentiating God from human values and products and prohibiting the worship of idols. It thus desacralized human values and opened the way for pluralism. Any deity that can be embodied in an idol must be rejected, because such a deity is not Yahweh.

The Secular City hymns the praises of the "secular city" and the process of secularization itself. That process ushers us into a new lifestyle that is quite different from that of tribal com-munities or more traditional towns. In the great urban centers of today's world we find anonymity, mobility, pragmatism, and a profane atmosphere. These qualities provide the best possi-ble atmosphere and context for the exercise of the respon-sibilities demanded by authentic biblical faith. Biblical faith, in turn, offers one of the best reasons for celebrating those fea tures of modern urban life and the process of secularization.

Today's secular city offers a set of characteristics and situa-tions that closely resemble those that confronted Jewish and Christian minorities in earlier days. Our response as believers should be to practice the faith as those earlier minorities did.

5853 4

Authentic faith in God radically differentiates the divine from the human, thereby according freedom to the human realm and compelling it to grow and develop on its own initiative. Cox insists that we must radically differentiate God from the world. He repeatedly uses such words as desacralization, deconsecration, exorcism, and disinterestedness. His point is that since the two realities are different, we have a religious responsibility toward the world. The church is the sign of the kingdom that is being built. As such it must try to discern God's activity in history so that it can collaborate with it. Rather than looking far in the future, however, the church should look around to see what is happening now so that its action may be fleshed out in the world. Thanks to the Bible, the church knows that Jesus was victorious over all principalities and powers, over all the forces opposed to human liberty: e.g., social classes, nationalism, ethnocentrism, and the sex drive.

Humankind and the world are free because God made them so. However history may unfold, it ultimately unfolds in accordance with God's plan. Fatalism is not the key because God has given us freedom. The Spirit blows where he wills, and the church must try to sense his presence in the happenings of this world. God's kingdom is never present here in all its fullness; it is always in the process of being built.[5]

I would also regard Gabriel Vahanian as one of the important theologians of secularization. In his view our present-day western culture based on technology is neither anti-Christian nor non-Christian; it is simply post-Christian. Our modern view of humanity, nature, and worldly reality is immanentist, scientific, and secular. It is diametrically opposed to the older and more traditional Christian view, which was transcendental, mythological, sacral, and sacramental, though of course the former did emanate from the latter.

In the eyes of modern, post-Christian people, God is neither necessary nor unnecessary. He is simply irrelevant and of no interest. It is as if God were dead. This is the thrust of Vahanian's book entitled *The Death of God,* which was published in 1960. In that work Vahanian criticizes the superficial religiosity of the postwar period, asserting that it was bound up with a conception of God as someone suited to our own measure.

Vahanian provides an in-depth analysis of the current situation of Christianity in western civilization, a civilization that has lost its awareness of God. People naturally tend toward some form of religiosity, says Vahanian. The problem today is that we have turned religion into a very distorted version of authentic biblical faith. We have substituted superstition for faith, turning religion into little more than a social or cultural phenomenon. Rather than embodying and expressing something that is of profound and vital interest, religion is simply a holdover. Having lost our authentic faith in God, we try to deceive ourselves by holding on to the tattered remnants of religion. Once it becomes institutionalized, faith becomes dogmatic and monolithic. It loses the qualities of doubt and risk that are essential components of authentic faith. Idolatrous and culturally defined concepts of God have replaced the biblical concept, and Christianity itself has been replaced by a superficial, superstitious, and syncretist religiosity: "We have domesticated God in such a way that, as *Waiting for Godot* seems to imply, he evaporates into a tragicomic mythological atavism; or he has become so diminutive as not to be recognizable any longer."[6]

On the basis of a broad and profound analysis of North American Protestantism, Vahanian concludes that we are living in a post-Christian era characterized by secular immanentism. This has given rise to a civil religiosity without authentic roots and to a practical idolatry devoid of authentic faith. The gap between the gospel message and today's practice of religion is greater than that which existed between Jerusalem and Athens, says Vahanian. Today's believers have turned faith and belief into an end in itself. The content of one's faith does not matter, and neither does God. People no longer think about God or the church or religious services. A purely formal and vacuous religiosity has killed the transcendent God of the Bible. Christian principles have lost their power; the gospel message no longer has any impact on people's practical lives. God has ceased to be important.

People today are not hostile to religion; they simply ignore it or live it in a routine way. The basic questions of religion no longer disturb them in the least. There is simply no room for real faith or religion in the scientific and technological outlook that dominates the post-Christian world. Modern religious practice is idolatrous, pseudo-religious, and pseudo-scientific. Genuine love and communion have been dropped for mere physical proximity and "togetherness." In that sense the proclamation of God's death may serve as a summons to return to a healthy and sound religiosity. In any case we must reject the emptiness and inauthenticity of religion as it is now practiced: "From this point of view, the death of God may be only a cultural phenomenon, as though only our religio-cultural notion of God were dead."[7]

Vahanian's book is really a protest against our murder of God and the humdrum routine of a desacralized world that is devoid of authentic values and has suffocated our inner life. Rather than theological reform, we need a cultural revolution, in Vahanian's opinion. We need a new language and a different sort of dialectics that will enable us to speak meaningfully of God once again and to drop our idolatry. We cannot prove the existence of God, but we should be able to sense that God must exist. God is not so much necessary as inevitable. God is the totally 'other' who is simultaneously present at all times. We need a profound and authentic faith in him today more than ever before.

In *Wait Without Idols* Vahanian suggests that we are now shaping a new concept of God and a new way of relating to him. A whole new kind of religiosity is in the making, and this suggests that we are entering a new era. But this new religiosity will rise on the tomb of a dead God.[8]

The positive contributions of this theology of secularization are clear and undeniable. It has pointed up the current distortion of religion and our misuse of God in trying to avoid our creative, transforming mission to the world. It has also laid the groundwork for a lifestyle that will take seriously the earthly and incarnational dimensions of faith.

At the same time, however, those theologians seemed to stop

halfway. The various theologies of secularization talked more about reform and transformation than about revolution; but revolution seems to be needed if we are to escape from the inhumanity of our technological world. They sought to present an alluring image of God to our atheistic world, but they did not really try to undermine the foundations of the practical atheism that characterizes the capitalist world today. Capitalist culture will never be able to accept the authentic divine image of Christian faith because the latter would completely subvert the values championed by the former.

The various theologies of secularization also failed to discover the essentially political dimension of faith and religion. They showed great naiveté in their attempts to analyze the existing structures and relationships based on oppression. Failing to realize that faith must begin by overthrowing a world based on inhumane technology and consumerism, they simply tried to show people how to live their faith in that world. They tried to undermine idolatry and get back to the biblical God, but they failed to realize that the biblical God manifests himself by liberating people from oppression and destroying oppressive societies. The fact is that we can escape from idolatry only when we accept the reality of a God who makes himself incarnate in the oppressed and then choose to stand on their side.[9]

The Theology of Hope

The theology of hope was another major effort to breathe new life into theology.[10] Building on the Marxist philosophy of Ernst Bloch[11] and the biblical conception of a God who keeps driving his people forward toward the future of his promise, Jürgen Moltmann elaborated a theology in which hope stood as the keystone of Christianity.[12] This hope is rooted in God's promise and in the resurrection of Christ, which serves as the guarantee and the fulfillment of that hope.

Christianity is eschatology, hope, a look directed toward the future; for that very reason it is also the opening up and the transformation of the present. . . . Christian faith draws its life from the resurrection of the crucified Christ and moves out toward the promises of Christ's universal future. . . . In the view of Christian eschatology, the future of man and the freedom of the sons of God and the future of creation as a whole are all kept open and defined by the future of the risen Christ and the promise that goes with it.[13]

This promise of resurrection, already fulfilled in Christ, gives Christian love the certainty of a future that will not fail. It needs that certainty if it is to be an "unfailing" love, if it is to combat the presence of suffering, evil, and death. It is in the hope of Christ's resurrection that Christian love overcomes the reality of death. For Christian hope, the end will come "only when the dead have been resurrected."[14]

Moltmann saw the danger that his theology might not have too much to contribute to the situation of those who are suffering from oppression here and now, precisely because it turns hope in the future into the central axis of Christian living. He tried to get around that difficulty, but he did not resolve it satisfactorily. He does insist that Christ is not only our consolation *in* suffering but also "the protest of God's promise *against* suffering."[15] Yet nowhere does he give concrete substance to this protest against evil in the present. While we have God's promise of triumphant resurrection, the power that crucified Christ still seems to reign supreme in the present.

The same criticism can be brought against him when he tries to show that Christian eschatological hope does not rob us of happiness in the present. His insistence is emotional and confident, but it also seems to be naive and ineffective in the last analysis. Indeed it is dangerous for any theology that claims to be committed to changing the present state of affairs, for it takes a pre-Marxist tack. The happiness of those suffering from poverty and oppression here and now lies in the promise of the parousia. The expectation of the parousia enables people "to accept everything in their present situation and to find joy in suffering as well as in happy events."[16] That sounds all too much like the old notion that the poor and oppressed should tranquilly accept their present lot because paradise awaits them.

In more than one respect, then, this theology of hope falls far short of the Christian view of faith as liberative action against oppression and injustice here and now. It seems incapable of concretizing its protest against oppression. It is likely to turn people into passive spectators who expect to be liberated by God in some distant future. It tends to equate human praxis with mere "obedience to God's promises." It has a naive view of the socio-political mechanisms of oppression, and it leaves them completely intact.[17] And it fails to realize that we can fashion the kingdom of God on earth only by actively fighting against oppression in the present.

Latin American Theology of Liberation[18]

Some Europeans are now saying that one must go to Latin America to learn any authentic theology today. Theologians like Harvey Cox have publicly acknowledged their debt to Gustavo Gutiérrez, and liberation theology has had a clear impact on the more recent stages of Metz's and Moltmann's thought.

I don't want to commit the sin of triumphalism by claiming that authentic theology is being done only in Latin America.[19] But since the Medellín Conference in 1968, there can be no doubt that Latin America has been in the forefront of a new and genuine theological movement that regards theology as critical reflection on historical praxis done in the light of Christian faith. In Latin America theology has taken to the streets. It has begun to reread and reinterpret the gospel message in terms of the concrete praxis of human beings committed to the process of human liberation. In the face of a long tradition that viewed theology as quiet reflection on the faith, there is now a vigorous and growing line of thought that sees theology as an active practice of the faith and critical reflection in the midst of that practice. In this section I should like to briefly discuss what I regard as the essential features of this new theology.

1. Liberation theology is rooted in Latin American realities. The first important feature of liberation theology is that it is markedly Latin American in character. It is clearly a Latin American phenomenon, the first major theological contribution from this oppressed and underdeveloped continent that is the home of more than one-third of all the Christians in the world. Its roots lie in the poor and needy, who have always been the epiphany of the Lord and who, for the most part, happen to be Christians in Latin America.

This new line of theological reflection is the expression of a new kind of Christianity that is being lived concretely and practiced ecumenically. Its practitioners include both Protestants (Rubem Alves, Julio de Santa Ana, Jorge Pixley, etc.) and Catholics (Gustavo Gutiérrez, Hugo Assmann, Enrique Dussel, Juan Luis Segundo, Gustavo Pérez Ramírez, Bezerra de Melo, etc.). It is also in active dialogue with Marxism, not through sterile debates and conferences, but through committed work for liberation in the realm of actual practice.

The language of liberation has arisen as a corollary to Latin America's new-found awareness of its dependence. The people of our continent have come to realize that they live in a state of dependence, not only politically, economically, and socially but also religiously and theologically. The affluent countries of the North Atlantic region make up the "dominating totality," to use the words of Enrique Dussel. They export not only their systems of domination but also the various philosophies and theologies that shore up those systems.

This fact is obvious enough in the case of those purely theoretical theologies that are blind to the reality of an oppressing and oppressed world (e.g., the theologies of such people as Küng, Pannenberg, and Dulles). But it holds true just as much, as we have seen, for other theologies that might seem to be more alluring: the theology of secularization (e.g., Gogarten and Cox); the theology of hope (Moltmann); the political theology of Johannes Metz; and even the ideologized theorizing about revolution and violence that has been so much in vogue in Europe. These latter theologies can be misleading because they seem to wear revolutionary dress. In fact their criticism is vague and ingenuous, and it never leaves the level of mere words. They are reformist theologies that simply do not go far enough. They have proved to be incapable of historical realism; they have failed to come down to earth and to offer concrete tactics and strategy. Since they reject only secondary features of the prevailing system and never place the whole system as such on trial, they can readily be absorbed by the mechanisms of the existing system of oppression.

Over against these theologies stands the theology of liberation. It presents itself as the Christian reflection of the dominated and oppressed world, which rejects the oppressing world in its totality. Starting off from human, social, and historical reality, it ponders the existing relationships based on injustice in a global frame and it also analyzes the mechanisms that are being used to keep the poor peoples of the world under domination. It is theological reflection on injustice in the light of Christian faith, but "it is elaborated with the help of the human sciences and on the basis of the concrete experiences and sufferings of the Latin American people."[20]

This does not mean that Latin America is advocating a ghetto Christianity or choosing to break completely with the churches of the North Atlantic region. The liberation dialectics in which it is enmeshed at present maintains that it is the liberation of the oppressed that will lead to the liberation of the oppressor *as well*. At this moment of history, Latin American Christianity in its state of dependence is looking for liberation in a process that will also salvage the Christianity causing its dependence. As Juan Luis Segundo puts it: "At this moment in history, when historical sensitivity and ecclesial flexibility are converging in Latin America as never before, this continent can be the fermenting-ground of a new conception of history, not only for itself but for Christianity. This new conception would start out from the Occident and a new idea of God that is closer to Christian revelation. And the two tasks may well be one."[21]

2. Liberation theology stresses orthopraxis over orthodoxy. A second essential element in this theology is its grounding in praxis. It defines itself as reflection on concrete action, on praxis, or as a secondary word whose first word is action. Praxis, the practical activity of Christians committed to the process of liberation, is the starting point that determines the critical content of this theology. Over against a theology of word or of abstract principles Latin America now posits a theology of lived faith, of committed action. Here a complete shift in view has taken place, and faith is understood as ortho-praxis rather than as orthodoxy. It is a faith viewed in terms of works, as Jesus and the prophets understood it.

Liberation theologians may well insist more on this point than on any other. Gustavo Gutiérrez, for example, stresses the "primacy" of action and regards liberative action as a "theological locus." Theology comes after. Framed in the con-text of praxis, it is "critical reflection" on that praxis.[22] The title of one of Segundo's books indicates clearly that he will move "from society to theology,"[23] that one can come to theology only from the real world of Latin America in its state of depen-dence and oppression. The same persistent stress on praxis pervades the work of Hugo Assmann. "Verbal formulations and writings are relevant only insofar as they are rooted in praxis," because "historical praxis is the basic aspect of faith."[24] Authentic theology must start off from committed activity to the cause of liberation, as the title of one of his more recent works indicates. It must be "theology from the praxis of liberation."[25]

3. Liberation theology chooses liberation over developmentalism. A third clear feature of liberation theology is its vigorous rejec-tion of developmentalist philosophies and theologies. The idiom and activity of the developmentalist approach will not suffice to solve the problems of the oppressed world because it is not simply a matter of effecting certain changes within the framework of the capitalistic economic system but rather of completely rejecting that system. Human liberation cannot be brought about by a developmentalist approach that maintains elitism and the relations of dependence and that ends up in the reifying atmosphere of a consumer culture. Lying hidden in the developmentalist approach is the yearning to maintain a world based on classes, privileges, and inhuman differences.

Gustavo Gutiérrez was the first to see this clearly. The initial formulation of his theology was based on a critical rejection of the oppressive tendencies underlying developmentalism:

Developmentalism thus came to be synonymous with *reformism* and modernization, that is to say, synonymous with timid measures, really ineffective in the long run and counterproductive to achieving a real transformation. The poor countries are becoming ever more clearly aware that their underdevelopment is only the by-product of the development of other countries, because of the kind of relationship which exists between the rich and the poor countries. Moreover, they are realizing that their own development will come about only with a struggle to break the domination of the rich countries. . . . Only a radical break from the status quo, that is, a profound transformation of the private property system, access to power of the exploited class, and a social revolution that would break this dependence would allow for the change to a new society, a socialist society—or at least allow that such a society might be possible.[26]

This concept of liberation is thoroughly biblical. Liberation theology articulates it as a process of liberation on three significant levels. First it is a process of socio-economic liberation for the oppressed peoples and social sectors of the world. Second, it is a process of liberation in which people gradually grow to maturity, accept their destiny and their vocation to be active subjects, and fashion a form of real, creative liberty in history. Third, it is a process of liberation from sin, which is the root of all evil, and which thereby paves the way for a life of full communion between all human beings and the Lord. This is a gift of God: the arrival of the kingdom. But we are obliged to proclaim it and hasten it by fighting against the structures of oppression that are concrete embodiments of sin.

4. Liberation theology chooses socialism. Another essential note of this theology, which is intimately bound up with the other features mentioned earlier, is its option for socialism. Socialism is regarded as the best social system for anyone who wants to live as a Christian, and it is therefore not surprising to see liberation theology spawning groups and movements advocating socialism: e.g., ONIS, ISAL, Golconda, Tercer Mundo, Christians for Socialism, and so forth. The same socialist orientation can be found in the two main journals that advocate the viewpoints of liberation theology: *Víspera* and *Cristianismo y Sociedad.*

Socialism is viewed as the first step and the precondition for the full and integral liberation of the oppressed. Any authentic process of liberation, which seeks to establish love and community between human beings, must begin with the foundation; and the foundation is justice. A world still marked by hunger, illiteracy, and stockpiling cannot allow people the right to indulge in affluence, luxury, and wastefulness. Human beings who place their own pleasure, caprice, and convenience over other people's chances to lead a decently human life are inhuman. The first step in the liberation process, therefore, must be a social revolution that will end oppression and dependence in order to establish an authentic socialism based on justice and equality.

But we must not make the mistake of thinking that the goals of liberation are solely economic. Its final aim is not an economic human being who no longer suffers from hunger and who has enough to live decently. Its final aim is a full and authentic human being in mind and heart and freedom. Liberation theology advocates a community of human beings who have both bread and liberty, who engage in dialogue rather than in silence or monologues, who live as beings with freedom rather than as beings under the fascism of possessiveness. It is a community in which property serves the interests of the majority, order serves liberty, and peace is subordinated to justice.

The conclusion is obvious enough. While liberation theology does posit socialism as a necessary preliminary step, it also transcends socialism. It is framed in the context of an ongoing revolution that will not stop until a communal world finds its definitive fulfillment in the kingdom of God.

5. Liberation theology affirms the class struggle. The theology of liberation arises out of the socio-economic realities of the world in which we are living. That obviously means a world filled with class struggle. Not to accept this fact is to choose not to see reality. To deny the slave's right to rebel in the name of some false peace is to take sides with the ongoing violence of the master. Not to side with the oppressed is to side with the oppressor.

Liberation theology confronts a class-ridden reality with the dialectics of practical Christian love, the norm that sums up the whole ethics of the gospel message. In a world marked by injustice and oppression, Christian love can be meaningful only as a revolutionary commitment to the liberation of one's fellow human beings. If love seeks a world of brothers and sisters, a world without classes, then it will fight for the liberation of the oppressed and fight against the enemy of the oppressed, trying to strip the latter of their status as oppressors and thereby make it possible for them to become real human beings. Love for the oppressors means fighting against them as oppressors in order to restore their nature as human beings to them. Thus with their combative love in quest of liberation, the oppressed also make it possible for the oppressor to be liberated and humanized. Revolutionary love makes it possible for two truly human beings to emerge where once there had been one oppressor and one oppressed.

This is the revolutionary dynamics of Christian love. For its appreciation of this dynamics, liberation theology is much indebted to Giulio Girardi, an Italian priest. Girardi has this to say:

The gospel commands us to love our enemies, but it does not say that we are not to oppose or fight them. Not only does love not rule out class struggle, it actually demands it. We cannot love the poor without lining up on their side in their struggle for liberation. . . . For the new Christian consciousness, class struggle is an imperative inextricably bound up with the commandment of love. It gives Christian love a new sense. Love is no longer static; it is dynamic and transforming. Its task is not only to recognize existing humanity but also to create the new humanity. . . . There is a new content in its universality. Universality is not neutrality. It implies a class option, an option for that class that carries with itself the interests of humanity and that will free the world in freeing itself. So we must love all, but not all in the same way. We love the oppressed by liberating them, the oppressors by fighting against them. We love the oppressed by liberating them from their wretched plight, the oppressors by liberating them from their sinfulness. Love must be class-oriented in order to be truly universal.[27]

Almost certainly influenced by Girardi, Gustavo Gutiérrez says practically the same thing:

The universality of Christian love is only an abstraction unless it becomes concrete history, process, conflict; it is arrived at only through particularity. To love all men does not mean avoiding confrontations; it does not mean preserving a fictitious harmony. Universal love is that which in solidarity with the oppressed seeks also to liberate the oppressors from their own power, from their ambition, and from their selfishness. . . . One loves the oppressors by liberating them from their inhuman condition as oppressors, by liberating them from themselves. But this cannot be achieved except by resolutely opting for the oppressed, that is, by combatting the oppressive class. . . . In the context of class struggle today, to love one's enemies presupposes recognizing and accepting that one has class enemies and that it is necessary to combat them. It is not a question of having no enemies, but rather of not excluding them from our love. But love does not mean that the oppressors are no longer enemies, nor does it eliminate the radicalness of the combat against them. "Love of enemies" does not ease tensions; rather it challenges the whole system and becomes a subversive formula.[28]

6. *Liberation theology has a profoundly prophetic thrust, in the biblical sense.* It is channelled in the same vein as prophecy at its most authentic. From the very midst of oppression it denounces the old oppressing order and proclaims the coming of a new liberating dispensation.

We have already considered the mission of the prophets. They stressed that authentic faith in Yahweh must be embodied in concrete acts of service to one's fellows. The social situation of the nation was clear and tangible proof of the inauthenticity or authenticity of their religious practices and their avowals of faith in Yahweh. A society pervaded by injustice and oppression was clearly an areligious society that Yahweh would reject, even though the odor of burnt offerings might fill the skies every day. The prophets did not just condemn the unjust world that they saw around them. Speaking in Yahweh's name, they predicted its tragic end in the near future. Darkness and destruction would not be Yahweh's last word, however, because a new order based on brotherhood would arise from the ashes of the old order based on oppression. Thus the prophet is sent by God "to root up and to tear down, to destroy and to demolish, to build and to plant" (Jer. 1:10).

Liberation theology echoes this prophetic dialectics of denunciation and annunciation. It is rooted in a praxis that says no to the world of oppression, but that stresses the annunciation of a new order that will arise out of the negation of a negating order. The affirmation of a new order can arise only out of the negation of the old order. This new order is the utopia glimpsed by the prophets: "They shall beat their swords into plowshares, and their spears into pruning hooks. One nation shall not raise the sword against another, nor shall they train for war again. Every man shall sit under his own vine, or under his own fig tree, undisturbed; for the mouth of the Lord of hosts has spoken (Mic. 4:3–4).

In the last analysis, both liberation theology and the prophets have the same vision. God's plan is one of hope and salvation, of justice and love. But first the enemies of love must be destroyed and oppressive structures must be eliminated. Yahweh will avenge his loved ones, and the dispossessed of the earth will inherit the kingdom of his peace. Then justice, the heart of authentic religion and the passionate concern of the prophets, will reign in the world.

If this is to happen, however, faith in the liberating God must become operative as a liberation praxis. To believe is not to make verbal affirmations but to work. Belief is a practical response to God's word, which itself is action: the liberating Word.

Notes

1. See D. Bonhoeffer, *Letters and Papers from Prison* (New York: Macmillan Paperback, 1962), p. 165; letter of April 30, 1944.

2. Ibid., letter of July 16, 1944, pp. 219–20.

3. John Robinson, *The New Reformation* (Philadelphia: Westminster Press, 1965), 106–22.

4. Harvey Cox, *The Secular City: Secularization and Urbanization in Theological Perspective* (New York: Macmillan, 1965), pp. 36 and 153.

5. Ibid., p. 116.

6. Gabriel Vahanian, *The Death of God* (New York: George Braziller, 1961), p. 54.

7. Ibid., p. 231.

8. G. Vahanian, *Wait Without Idols* (New York: George Braziller, 1964).

9. The death of God movement, as advocated by Hamilton, Paul Van Buren, and Altizer, was a distortion of the theology of secularization. It advocated a Christian atheism, a wholly unconvincing blend of secular humanism and an idealized portrait of the man named Jesus of Nazareth. This blend convinced neither atheists nor Christians, and hence the movement was short-lived.

10. We must mention, if only briefly, the particular contribution of J.B. Metz and his political theology. For Metz, faith clearly has a political dimension. Belief in God entails a definite commitment to the process of creating a better and more humane world. An exclusivist faith that is wholly absorbed in the individual believer's dialogue with God makes no sense in today's world. In the Thou of God, believers must embrace the whole of humanity. Their faith in God must be translated into love for their neighbor. To be sincere in our inhuman world, this love must be converted into a revolutionary commitment to fashion a better world: "Love must be interpreted and acted upon in its social dimension. This means that love must be interpreted as an unconditional commitment to the cause of justice, liberty, and peace for others. . . . Understood thus, Christian love can call for a truly revolutionary commitment. When the social *status quo* is rife with injustice, a revolution on behalf of justice and liberty for 'the least of our brothers' certainly cannot be ruled out in the name of love" (*Theology of the World*, Eng. trans. [New York: Seabury, 1969], pp. 119–20).

This dimension of love clearly produces a revolutionary ferment. Metz insists that Christianity must recapture its originally "subversive" elements of content that challenge every oppressive structure. The same dynamic should turn the church into an institution of "social criticism." Free from all partisanship and compromise with the power structure, the church must join with the prophets of old in protesting against every kind of oppression and dehumanization, be it economic, political, social, ideological, or religious.

While Metz certainly makes a definite contribution, he failed to give concrete expression to his criticism of the mechanisms of oppression. He also failed to see that the capitalist system does not simply cause certain injustices but is actually unjust and inhuman in its totality. Furthermore, Metz did not offer any concrete elaboration of tactics or strategy. As Assmann puts it, Metz seems to be afraid "to name the mechanisms of oppression." Thus his theology remains merely reformist, and it can be readily assimilated by the existing system. As we shall see, Latin American theology of liberation tries to face up to these difficulties and fill in these gaps.

11. Ernst Bloch is the chief spokesman for a revised version of the Marxist tradition. Seeking to get beyond the narrow confines of the Leninist and Stalinist systems, Bloch wants to go back to the pre-Marxist sources of prophetic history and the politico-religious manifestations of the western world's revolutionary history. He is interested in the spirit of unrest that has driven humanity forward toward the future, the hope of some new future that has held us in check and pushed us forward throughout history. As Bloch sees it, religion (and also fantasy, dreams, and mysticism) need not simply be a cause of alienation; it may also go to the very heart of being human. Religious awareness takes in human needs, motives, and "spheres" which are indeed associated with socio-economic revolution but which certainly cannot be explained on that basis alone. Bloch thinks there has been too much talk about

economic life but not enough about human life. The meaning of humanity is not exhausted in socio-economic analyses and explanations. Even after we have said everything there is to be said about social and economic roots, the human being remains an unanswered question. We are a process, *homo absconditus*, beings that "together with the surrounding world are both a task and an enórmous receptacle laden with the future." We remain in the ongoing tension of our "not yet," our struggle for complete fulfillment. Bloch wants Marxism to find its teleological thread, the thread that will save it from fixism and dogmatism. This thread is essentially religious, says Bloch, because the mission of religion is to keep alive our expectation for the new, for the future that is our God.

12. See Jürgen Moltmann, *Teología de la esperanza*, Spanish trans. (Salamanca: Sígueme, 1969); Eng. trans.: *Theology of Hope* (New York: Harper & Row, 1967): "The God in question . . . is the 'God of hope' (Rom. 15:13); a God whose character is constituted by the future. . . . The God of the Exodus and the Resurrection 'is' not an eternal present; he promises his presence and proximity to those who follow his lead into the future. YHWH is the name of a God who primarily promises his presence and his kingdom, and who situates man in expectation of the future. YHWH is a God whose constitutive character is the future, a God whose freedom triggers the new that is to come" (p. 38).

13. Moltmann, ibid., pp. 20 and 441.

14. Ibid., p. 460.

15. Ibid., p. 29.

16. Ibid., p. 40.

17. For more details, one can consider the criticisms made of this theology by Rubem Alves, *Religión: ¿Opio o instrumento de liberación?* (Montevideo: Tierra Nueva, 1970), pp. 99–100. Also, and even more importantly, see Hugo Assmann, *Opresión-liberación: Desafío a los cristianos* (Montevideo: Tierra Nueva, 1971), pp. 80–81 and 120–21. Assmann's basic point of view can be seen clearly in the translated volume *Theology for a Nomad Church* (Maryknoll, New York: Orbis Books, 1976).

18. I realize that the expression "theology of liberation" is or should be redundant, since any authentic theology ought to be basically liberative. Authentic theology is supposed to be discourse on a God who has chosen to reveal himself as our liberator. But I retain the term "liberation theology" to distinguish the current theological trend in Latin America from the transformist theologies of the pseudo-Christian civilization of the western technological world.

19. Here I shall let a European theologian spell out the difference between current Latin American theology and European theology: "Even when it has not yet found a popular idiom, Latin American theology is born in the people and of the people, and it is born of a real, concrete commitment. It is similar to the reflection that Moses engaged in when he went off by himself at stopping points in the Exodus. It is similar to the reflection to which Jeremiah was driven when he realized that he must either be with his people or a stranger among them. For that reason there is a substantive difference in language and symbol between European theology and that of Latin America.

"European theology is opening up to the people and moving *toward* earthly realities and their history; Latin American theology is *in* the people and their history. This point can be confused greatly because European theology has become bold and unprejudiced. Like an old aristocracy that does not want to lose its right to live and make its presence felt in the world, modern theology is engaged in all sorts of ventures: the theology of change, the theology of revolution, the theology of violence, and so forth. We may soon look for 'the theology of Coca-Cola.' All this represents the effort of people who do not want to lose their observation post and their right to judge the world without moving out of their armchairs or their libraries. I don't know why it is taking us so long to realize that our European theology is not accompanying history as it happens. It follows history and judges it when that history has already entered eternity.

"European theologians cannot possibly understand the wellsprings of Latin American theology until they realize that the two factions are talking about earth, but that one faction is talking about the earth before Copernicus and the other is talking about the earth after Copernicus. It is a realization that they should arrive at soon. From its faith European theology deduces a political vision which has cut the thorny knot of Marxism but which can never completely forget that it is a prefixed political position wholly separated from the competing strands of real history. Hence it is doomed to be an 'intermediary' politics of conciliation. Christian Democratic politicians, be they Caldera or Frei, never really get beyond an Adenauer or a De Gasperi in understanding and carrying through the Latin American revolution (though Maritain considers the Chilean as one of the three best revolutionaries on earth). Even at their best they are products of a Christian training that has prepared people, not to read and interpret history, but to offer a counterproposal to history; not to describe a God who guides human history, but to defend the 'rights of God.'

"Latin American theology is discovering that faith is *intrinsically political* because adhering to Christ simultaneously means establishing a vital relationship with the Father and being responsible for 'others' in real life. It means entering into a poor, oppressed family that cannot wait any longer, that urgently needs liberation. It may well be possible that Latin American and European theologians might well agree on the definition of faith as intrinsically political. The substantive difference between them is to be found in their completely different concrete situations. Latin America does not have any theological tradition to defend, nor any commitment to apologetics. Its people have already rejected certain ideologies, not through a process of controversy and debate but through an inability to assimilate them. Here theology really is in a position to become a biblical, prophetic theology. It has no need of a theology of revolution, or a theology of violence, or a theology of secular realities, as we are wont to encounter these lines of thought. Latin American theology centers around reflection on real happenings in the light of God's word. It seeks to discover God in the people, in taking cognizance of dependence and potential initiatives on behalf of liberation" (Arturo Paoli, "Latinoamérica: Explosivo continente del futuro," *SIC* 36 [June 1973]: 273).

20. E. Dussel, *América Latina, Dependencia y liberación* (Buenos Aires: Cambeiro, 1973), p. 218.

21. J. L. Segundo, *Our Idea of God,* Eng. trans. (Maryknoll, New York: Orbis Books, 1974), pp. 36–37 (Vol. 3 of *Theology for Artisans of a New Humanity*). See also his work, *The Liberation of Theology* (Maryknoll, New York: Orbis Books, 1976).

22. Gustavo Gutiérrez, *A Theology of Liberation,* Eng. trans. (Maryknoll, New York: Orbis Books, 1973); see Chapter 1, pp. 6–13.

23. J.L. Segundo, *De la sociedad a la teología* (Buenos Aires: Ed. Carlos Lohle, 1972); also *The Liberation of Theology.*

24. Hugo Assmann, *Opresión-liberación: Desafío a los cristianos,* pp. 21 and 32.

25. H. Assmann, *Teología desde la praxis de liberación* (Salamanca: Sígueme, 1973); in English see *Theology for a Nomad Church.*

26. Gustavo Gutiérrez, *A Theology of Liberation,* Chapter Two, pp. 26–27. See also Gustavo Pérez Ramírez, "Liberation: A Recurring Prophetic Cry in the Americas," in *Freedom and Unfreedom in the Americas,* ed. Thomas E. Quigley, CICOP, U.S.Catholic Conference (New York: IDOC, 1971). In that work the author, a Colombian theologian, maintains that genuine development means something very different from the integration of the marginated people into the capitalist system of consumer society. Genuine development must be a liberation from that very system (ibid., pp. 1–3).

In a similar vein Denis Goulet sees "development" as the linguistic embodiment of the domination exercised by the most affluent and powerful societies. Oppressed groups cannot be liberated through the developmental approach because this approach allows those in power to maintain strict control over the process of development ("Development or Liberation," CICOP, Washington, D.C., 1971, p. 2).

27. Giulio Girardi, "Cristianismo y lucha de clases," *Razón y Fe,* 872–73 (September–October 1970), p. 251; paper originally delivered at the fifth Theology Week, University of Deusto, 1969.

28. Gustavo Gutiérrez, *Theology of Liberation,* pp. 275–76. Jean Cardonell speaks in almost identical terms: "There is no more forceful gesture of love for one's enemies than destroying their privileged elitist position and thus ushering them into the immense joy of a common, shared condition. . . . If I am to live out the new commandment of fraternal love for the great landowners of Latin America, I must take part in the great struggle to dispossess them" ("Amor creador y revolución," in Julio Colomer, "Apuntes bibliográficos sobre teología de la revolución," *Razón y Fe,* No. 872–73 [September–October 1970] pp. 231–57).

Moltmann, too, considers revolution to be a gesture of love for both the oppressors and the oppressed. Commenting on Camus's understanding of the humane principle underlying rebellion and revolution, he says: "The slave rebels against his master. He rejects the master as master, but not as a human being. As slave and master respectively, neither of the two are truly human beings. If the slave were to deny his master as a human being, he would not usher anything new into the world; it would simply be a reversal of roles. But the aim of human revolution is to abolish the existing slave-master relationship so that all that will exist afterwards will be equality between human beings. When the revolution loses sight of this end, it turns into nihilism. Thus when Christians take sides with the 'wretched of the earth,' they are looking for the redemption of both them and their oppressors. Only through this dialectic can the universality of the crucified one turn into a reality." So we can never forget that "the duty of all who love truly is to make revolution; the obligation of every revolutionary is to practice love" (Jürgen Moltmann, "Gott in der Revolution," *Selecciones de Teología* 31 [1969]: 246–48; in English see "God in the Revolution," in Moltmann's *Religion, Revolution and the Future* [New York: Scribner's, 1969]).

PART III

TOWARD A DIALOGUE WITH ATHEISM

In this final section of the book I should like to take the first steps toward a dialogue with the main strands of atheism, using the perspectives opened up by liberation theology as a starting point. Needless to say, I am referring here to various kinds of humanistic atheism, to those that feel obliged to reject God as an impediment to human greatness.

I don't want to give the reader the idea that I am wholly naive. I am not at all suggesting that the whole blame for atheism is to be found in the false conception of God that has been presented by Christianity. I fully realize that even with the best possible theology we will have countless atheists. But that does not stop me from joining forces with atheism to attack as idolatrous all those conceptions of God that diminish human greatness or block human liberation. I, too, am an atheist when it comes to the God that is rejected by most atheists!

I am convinced that if people did feel the need to attack God in order to liberate humanity, it was precisely because people had totally lost sight of God as liberator.

In this age of alienation and dehumanization, we should not spend too much time worrying about the death of God. God is

7

THE PROPHET OF ATHEISTIC HUMANISM: NIETZSCHE

The Madman. . . "Whither is God" he cried. "I shall tell
you. We have killed him you and I. All of us are his
murderers. But how have we done this? How were we able
to drink up the sea? Who gave us the sponge to wipe away
the entire horizon? What did we do when we unchained
this earth from its sun? Whither is it moving now? Whither
are we moving now? Away from all suns? Are we not
plunging continually? Backward, sideward, forward, in
all directions? Is there any up or down left? Are we not
straying as through an infinite nothing? Do we not feel the
breath of empty space? Has it not become colder? Is not
night and more night coming on all the while? Must not
lanterns be lit in the morning? Do we not hear anything yet
of the noise of the gravediggers who are burying God?"
—The Gay Science, 125, Kaufmann trans.

Modern atheism found its major prophet in Friedrich
Nietzsche. With an explosive style and an impetuous rush of
thought ranging from sacrilege to mysticism, Nietzsche
prophetically proclaimed that God was dead and that we
human beings had killed him. Moreover, for Nietzsche proc-

lamation of the death of God was an essential preliminary to human liberation. We had to will and to declare God's death. And because Nietzsche fully appreciated the transcendent import of his proclamation, it has a heart-rending ring to it: "The greatest recent event—that 'God is dead,' that the belief in the Christian God has ceased to be believable—is even now beginning to cast its first shadows over Europe. For the few, at least, whose eyes, whose *suspicion* in their eyes, is strong and sensitive enough for this spectacle, some sun seems to have set just now. . . ."[1]

The phrase "God is dead" would soon turn into a cliché. But when Nietzsche put it in the mouth of Zarathustra, it represented only half of his message. The other half was: "I come to teach you the Overman." To Nietzsche, one half of the message did not make any sense without the other. The Overman was to take the place of a dead God. Zarathustra was entrusted with the task of conveying the news of God's death to the world. As he starts on his journey, he meets an old hermit, a saint. The saint tells Zarathustra that he himself loves God but not man, because man is too imperfect. Zarathustra replies that he loves man, and then he asks the saint what he is doing in the forest. The saint replies: "I make songs and sing them; and when I make songs, I laugh, cry, and hum: thus I praise God." The two separate, laughing like young boys. But when Zarathustra is alone again, he wonders to himself: "Could it be possible? This old saint in the forest has not yet heard anything of this, that *God is dead!*"[2]

Before enthroning the Overman, therefore, Zarathustra must go through the world announcing the news of the death of God, for that God is permitting vain and futile lives. A world without God cannot go on being inhabited by petty human beings. The void once filled with the divine presence must now give rise to the Overman. Ultimately God is what people need to be more human. Hence the advent of the Overman will take place only when the world openly recognizes and wholeheartedly proclaims the death of God and when human beings have usurped God's qualities.

The basic principle of Nietzsche's whole philosophy, and

hence of his atheism, is the will to power. For Nietzsche there are only two kinds of human beings: the powerful and the weak. Only the powerful have a right to existence since life is struggle, force, domination—the will to power.[3] Over against Schopenhauer's pessimism and its concomitant need for salvation, and also over against the artistic ideal that Nietzsche saw embodied in the personality of Wagner, Nietzsche himself set up the will to power. In the struggle for existence, among human beings as in the jungle, the weak die off. A real and authentic human being is characterized by his struggle to attain power rather than happiness. Happiness is rather static and simple-minded; it leads to decadence. Only a life of risk, effort, and danger is human, and such a life will entail suffering, abandonment, scorn, and confident trust. Authentic man, strong and powerful, is merely a bridge between animal and Overman.

To abet the coming of the Overman, who is already on the way, we must declare the death of God. We must also declare the death of the morality that impedes his coming by championing the virtues of the weak. "The saint who pleases God," says Nietzsche, "is a castrated ideal. . . . Life ends where the kingdom of God begins." The virtues of the Overman stand in radical opposition to the Christian virtues. We must have done with Christianity and its God, a God who defends the weak and the petty. The idea of human equality is intolerable to Nietzsche. He maintains that it was invented by those weak pygmies, the fishermen of Galilee, who were chilled by the grandeur of the Roman Empire. Moreover, faith in divine providence robs people of their motivation to fight for a better future. They give up their thirst for power and get drunk on passivism. Indeed, to put it in general terms, all the virtues preached by Christianity are the most radical negation of authentic human life. If the Overman is to live, then we must have the death of the Christian God who demands and guarantees those debilitating virtues. God, then, is dead and the Overman will live to take his place.

There has been much debate as to what Nietzsche meant in proclaiming the death of God. What does Zarathustra have in mind as he sets out to convince the world that God is really dead? Does he want to free people from a false superstition, as Sartre thinks? Does he simply want to bear witness to spiritual aridity, as Heidegger thinks? Does he simply want to point up God's withdrawal from the world, as Buber thinks? Or is Zarathustra the new Christ, who prompts us to live a full life by proclaiming the death of the gods in his own flesh?

I think all these interpretations go a bit too far and need not be accepted. I would agree with Gilson that Nietzsche's notion of the death of God is essentially an ethical notion.[4] He is basically out to work a reform, to eliminate the Judeo-Christian ideal of humility, charity, and submissiveness and exalt the notions of power and strength. In short, he wants to exalt all human powers to their highest level. What is dead is the Christian God of traditional ethics. He is opposed to Christian principles and their "will to nothingness" more than he is opposed to God. We must reject Christian morality as a "capital crime" against life; otherwise its defenders will have every chance of coming out on top. Christian morality is an anti-humanism. It has debased the notion of many by attributing all that is best in man to God, thus depriving man of his power and his love.

Nietzsche's sharpest attacks are against the meek, the pure of heart, the lowly, and the poor. He feels we must abominate an ideal which preaches virtues that are directly opposed to the will to power and the virtues of the Overman, and his war on Christianity is waged most clearly in *The Antichrist.*

Of course Nietzsche was not the first person to reject the God grounded in Christian principles as the very negation of life. In the early Renaissance period, Machiavelli declared war on Christianity for making happiness consist in "humility and scorn for human powers and virtues." In the eighteenth century the circle of thinkers around Diderot and Baron D'Holbach also attacked Christianity for much the same reasons. Grimm, too, attacked it for preaching ignominy, humility, and servitude. He asserted that "the Spirit of the Gospel has never been able to go hand in hand with the principles of good government."[5]

Yet it was Nietzsche who preached this aversion to Christianity most forcefully and drew its ultimate consequences. If we aspire to greatness, we must reject a God who demands submission and debasement. In his *Prologue (Thus Spoke Zarathustra,* Part I) Zarathustra says: "Once the sin against God was the greatest sin; but God died, and these sinners died with him" *(Portable Nietzsche,* p. 125). Now to sin against the earth and man is the worst sin, and we do that by attributing greater importance to heaven and God than to the earth and man. That is why Nietzsche ends *The Antichrist* with this declaration: "I call Christianity the one great curse, the one great innermost corruption, the one great instinct of revenge, for which no means is poisonous, stealthy, subterranean, *small* enough—I call it the one immortal blemish of mankind" *(Portable Nietzsche,* p. 656).

If we want to liberate people from the idea of God, that "undesirable quest," we should not worry too much about refuting the proofs for his existence. Instead we should replace Christian values with other values that will exalt human beings rather than degrading them. Thus Nietzsche's atheism is really an anti-Christian stance rather than atheism in the strict sense. It is a rejection of an ethics that champions weakness, simple-mindedness, and pettiness. His anti-Christian stance is a decision, an act of choice based on personal preference rather than arguments, as he himself noted. The death of God is not so much something to be proved as a choice to be made and then proclaimed. As Jean Wahl puts it: "It is not so much a terrible act as something positively willed by him."[6] To proclaim the death of God is to free oneself from weakness and pettiness. We become the murderers of God by turning our backs on God and saying no to the virtues and principles God demands.

At the bottom of Nietzsche's atheism there is clearly a great yearning to liberate people from a whole series of principles that he regards as inhuman. We have good reason to imagine that Nietzsche would have been attracted by the idea of a God who wills and seeks human greatness, who rejects passivity and inaction, who does not like to see the soul of a slave and keeps prodding people on toward liberation. It is a fact that Nietzsche evinced an almost religious fervor for Dionysus, the Greek god of wine and drunken ecstasy, who brought all human beings together in the joy of festive celebration. Dionysus is the God who rejects asceticism and obligation, who is indifferent to good and evil, and whom Nietzsche described as "the rightful name of the Antichrist" when he later added "An Attempt at Self-Criticism" to *The Birth of Tragedy*. For Nietzsche, Dionysian art is a hymn to the pleasure of existence, a frenzy of life and joy, of overcoming and triumph. Eventually the figure of Dionysus becomes a fusion of the two Greek gods, Apollo and Dionysus, and it is that fusion to which Nietzsche refers when he calls himself "Dionysus" in *Ecce Homo*.

I am not trying to suggest that Nietzsche would have accepted Yahweh if Yahweh were presented in Dionysian terms. The fact is that Yahweh, the liberator God, begins by liberating people from the fund of haughtiness and egotism that Nietzsche hoped to use as the basis for his religion. The liberator God wants human greatness, but he does not want it for only a few privileged souls whose power will be based on the exploitation of the weak. He wants all humanity to be free, great, and strong in the ties of communion and love. The cult of Dionysus would return us to the jungle, restoring the principle that might makes right. The liberator God does not want some people to be neglected and downtrodden as Nietzsche thought. He wants people to be strong and combative, athirst for liberty, and in fellowship with each other.

While Nietzsche's atheism is violent and absolute, perhaps even pathological in *Ecce Homo,* it is nevertheless true that it is primarily an attack on the distortion of Christianity. It is a denunciation of Jesus as a man of humility and suffering, as a preacher of an ideal that entails the rejection of this world. People must remain "faithful to the earth," and so Nietzsche attacks a morality and a God that command human beings to be concerned mainly about heaven.

In all likelihood Nietzsche would have only scorn for many of the people who consider themselves his disciples, who go through the world proclaiming the death of God but living the empty lives of simpletons. As he himself put it in *Thus Spoke Zarathustra,* some people will topple images and statues and claim that nothing is worthy of veneration because they themselves are incapable of forming themselves and creating their image of God.[7] If atheism does not give rise to an even more radical humanism and a life fraught with freedom and riskiness, then it makes no sense. God is to be rejected because he is the embodiment and bulwark of inhuman values.

We can readily understand Nietzsche's view of Christianity and its God insofar as he saw them as the advocates of pettiness and weakness. But Nietzsche failed to understand them and took them wrongly. To him being a Christian meant being weak, fleeing from battle, hiding in the face of danger, despising this world and thinking only about the happiness of heaven. We can understand much of what Nietzsche says if we appreciate his justifiable reaction against such an attitude and his passionate nature, which gave way to pathology in the final years of his life.

At bottom Nietzsche never was an atheist. He was brutally anti-Christian, or better perhaps, brutally anti-weak. He was a great defender of humankind. He wanted people to be great and strong, to measure up to the grandiose vision of his own passionate nature. In an age when Christianity was being lived as a force for alienation and domestication, it is not surprising that Nietzsche should rebel against it; and it is understandable that he might go to the opposite extreme.

Toward the end of his study of Nietzsche's philosophy, Karl Jaspers remarks that the transcendental nihilism regarding existence embraced by Nietzsche brought him nothing, certainly not peace. Thus his so-called atheism is rather a restless and increasingly poignant search for God. At an early age Nietzsche penned a poem, a prayer to "the unknown God." In it he struggles against the relentless pursuit of God and at the same time proclaims his decision to serve him. Later Nietzsche would roundly reject God, but he was never able to free himself fully from the pursuit he had experienced as a young man. A blasphemous rebel, his temperament and his honesty did not permit him to accept a God to whom downtrodden and defeated masses prayed; he sought fulfillment in the fervent strains of the Dionysian cult and preached the Overman.

As life went on, however, his heart-rending solitude grew deeper and deeper. So did the fearsome and depressing image of a world without God. If God is dead, then we can no longer pray or worship or rest confidently in some ultimate Power or Truth. We live alone without friends and without hope on a mountain-top covered with snow. With God dead there is no final recompense, no place where the heart can find rest. Without God there is no morality, the shadow of nihilism covers the earth, all is vanity, and we are reduced to the category of mere animals. In *The Antichrist* he says: "We no longer derive man from 'the spirit' or 'the deity'; we have placed him back among the animals" (*Portable Nietzsche,* p. 580).

Pascal had thought that without the Christian faith people would turn into monsters and nature into chaos. Nietzsche agrees with that estimate and in his notes for *The Will to Power* he claims to have fulfilled that prophecy.[8]

Overtaken by fear and loneliness, Nietzsche opted eventually to summon God back again. In marvelous language he decribes the nostalgia for God as a shadow nailed to Zarathustra's heels. If Zarathustra is an idealized image of Nietzsche himself, then the shadow that pursues Zarathustra is the image of God that Nietzsche was never able to rid himself of completely. His cry to God has surprisingly mystical undertones:

> Away!
> He himself fled,
> My last, only companion,
> My grcat cncmy,
> My unknown,
> My hangman-god.
>
> No! Do come back
> With all thy tortures!

To the last of all that are lonely,
Oh, come back!
All my tear-streams run
Their course to thee;
And my heart's final flame—
Flares up for thee!
Oh, come back,
My unknown god! My *pain!*
My last—happiness!"[9]

Nietzsche vehemently proclaimed the death of God. Throughout his life he rejected and rebelled against the Christian qualities that diminished human beings. Kierkegaard, by contrast, is a philosopher who opted heart and soul for the God of Christianity. Yet these two men shared many traits in common. Both were passionate individualists, subjective in their thinking and hostile to Hegelianism. Both were assiduous readers of Schopenhauer, tragic and demanding loners of great personality. Confronted with the very same problem, however, they chose to move in very different directions. Nietzsche became the prophet of the death of God. Kierkegaard chose to become the passionate witness of total surrender to God. His life bore courageous witness to a sincere and solid faith that led him to attack the official Christianity of the Danish church for its superficiality, soft-headedness, and lack of sincerity and depth. Kierkegaard's critical and passionate faith, his "Archimedes' point," is often fraught with pain and obscurity, but it is always staunch, radical, and aggressive. It is the best response to the ceaselessly rebellious sorrow and groping of Nietzsche.

Kierkegaard saw the faults of Christianity and attacked them, trying to become more and more Christian all the time. Nietzsche, too, saw the failings and went on to generalize them. He would passionately attack anything that even smacked of Christianity. His rejection of it was systematic, passionate, and total. And for that very reason it was superficial,[10] if not downright contradictory. André Gide said this about him:

In the presence of the gospel Nietzsche's immediate and profound reaction was—it must be admitted—jealousy. It does not seem to me that Nietzsche's work can be really understood without allowing for that feeling. Nietzsche was jealous of Christ, jealous to the point of madness. In writing his *Zarathustra* Nietzsche was continually tormented with the desire to contradict the gospel. Often he adopted the actual form of the Beatitudes in order to reverse them. He wrote *Anti-Christ,* and in his last work, *Ecce Homo,* set himself up as the victorious rival of Him whose teaching he proposed to supplant.[11]

Kierkegaard adopted a diametrically opposed attitude. In his eyes the person had meaning only as "a subject in relation to God." Christianity was his grand passion. He chose to believe, and pursued the consequences of that faith to the very end. So in Nietzsche and Kierkegaard we see two people whose lives gravitated around the person of Christ. So similar and yet so different, they are identical at bottom. Both rose up in rebellion against a lifeless brand of Christianity. Both sought to bring salvation to people. But where one chose hatred, the other championed love. Yet love and hatred can signify the same thing.

Notes

1. F. Nietzsche, *The Gay Science*, 343; Eng. trans., *The Portable Nietzsche*, trans. Walter Kaufmann (New York: Viking Press, 1968), p. 96.

2. F. Nietzsche, *Thus Spoke Zarathustra*, First Part, *The Portable Nietzsche*, pp. 123–24.

3. See his notes collected in *The Will to Power*, Eng. trans., Walter Kaufmann (New York: Vintage Books, 1968).

4. See the article by E. Gilson, "The Idea of God and the Difficulties of Atheism," *The Great Ideas Today* (Chicago: Encyclopaedia Britannica, 1969), p. 241.

5. Grimm, "Correspondance Literaire," cited by H. de Lubac in *The Drama of Atheistic Humanism*, Eng. trans. (New York: Meridian Books, 1963), p. 65.

6. Jean Wahl, "Le Nietzsche de Jaspers," *Recherches Philosophiques*, Vol. VI, p. 356.

7. F. Nietzsche, *Thus Spoke Zarathustra*, Third Part; see "On Old and New Tablets."

8. See. F. Nietzsche, *The Will to Power*.

9. F. Nietzsche, *Thus Spoke Zarathustra*, Fourth Part, p. 367.

10. In *Ecce Homo*, for example, Nietzsche wrote: "I do not by any means know atheism as a result; even less as an event: it is a matter of course with me, from instinct." He tells us that such notions as "God," "immortality of the soul," and "redemption" were concepts to which he never "devoted any attention, or time; not even as a child." Elsewhere in the same book he tells us that the question of God's existence is far less important than the question of diet ("Why I Am So Clever"). See *Ecce Homo*, Eng. trans.: Walter Kaufmann, *Basic Writings of Nietzsche* (New York: Random House, 1968), p. 692.

11. Comment of André Gide, cited by H. de Lubac, *The Drama of Atheistic Humanism*, p. 180.

8

GOD AS ILLUSION: FEUERBACH, FREUD, RUSSELL

The divine being is nothing else than the human being, or, rather, the human nature purified, freed from the limits of the individual man, made objective—i.e., contemplated and revered as another, a distinct being.

—Feuerbach

Religion is the universal obsessional neurosis of humanity.
—Freud

The natural sciences, the one and only source of information and knowledge, offer no basis at all for faith in God.
—Russell

Ludwig Feuerbach

At the close of his lectures in Heidelberg, Feuerbach spelled out his own chief desire and aspiration.[1] It was to change "the friends of God into friends of man, believers into thinkers, worshippers into workers, candidates for the other world into students of this world, Christians, who on their own confession are half-animal and half-angel, into men—whole men."[2]

His own doctrine, then, is quite clear: Theology is simply anthropology. The object of religion, which we call God, is simply an expression of the human essence. We must reject our false illusions about God and recapture the qualities that are properly our own as human beings.

In his early youth Feuerbach was a fervent believer. He himself acknowledged that God was his first and foremost thought. He began the study of theology in Heidelberg with the intention of being ordained a Protestant minister. Then he transferred to Berlin, which became his "spiritual cradle." Taking up the study of Hegel, who became his "second father," Feuerbach soon became convinced that the existence of God could not be proved rationally. He went on to deny the existence of God altogether. The only mission left to him was to prove to believers that God is simply an illusion, a projection of the qualities we find in human nature itself. Like a drunkard in front of a mirror, the believer sees an imaginary double image when, in fact, only one real person exists. The mission of philosophy, then, is to restore humankind to sobriety through a sincere and satisfactory critique of religion.

In the Preface to the second edition of *The Essence of Christianity* Feuerbach stresses that the distinction between the divine and the human is an illusion. This means that both the object and the teaching of Christianity are merely human. The divinity of nature is the foundation of all religions, including Christianity; and their final goal must be the divinization of human beings. History will reach a major turning point when human beings fully realize that their one and only God is they themselves: *"Homo homini Deus."* Love between human beings must be elevated to the level of the divine, for they are the beginning, middle, and end of all religion.[3]

Feuerbach dedicated all his energy to proving this in his various works. In his *Reflection on Death and Immortality* he tried to show that our idea of immortality is simply a consoling self-deception designed to help us avoid the fact that the dead really *are dead.* The same sharp criticism and genial probing can be found in his two best known works: *The Essence of Christianity* and *The Essence of Religion.*[4]

The starting point for Feuerbach's philosophizing is concrete, material human beings here and now. God and Absolute Spirit, the objects of Hegel's speculations, would be seen to be simply projections of human qualities and characteristics into another illusory world. The statements of religion about God are the illusory dreams of individuals who project their own being into an abstract idea. The real object of religion is the essence of the individual, and human beings are their own God. Says Feuerbach: "It is not I, an insignificant individual, but religion itself that says: God is man, man is God; it is not I, but religion that denies the God who is *not* man, but only an *ens rationis*."[5]

Feuerbach has no intention of saying that God is nothing at all. His point is that God is not what the web of theological illusions makes him out to be. God is indeed a mystery, but this mystery is not alien to human nature; indeed it has to do with human nature itself. God is human qualities imagined as infinite and personified in a concept:

The object of any subject is nothing else than the subject's own nature taken objectively. Such as are a man's thoughts and dispositions, such is his God. . . . By his God thou knowest the man, and by the man his God; the two are identical. . . . God is the manifested inward nature, the expressed self of a man—religion the solemn unveiling of a man's hidden treasures, the revelation of his intimate thoughts, the open confession of his love secrets. . . . The divine being is nothing else than the human being, or, rather, the human nature purified, freed from the limits of the individual man, made objective—i.e., contemplated and revered as another, a distinct being. All the attributes of the divine nature are, therefore, attributes of the human nature.[6]

From that point of view it is clear that faith in God impoverishes us. For God's very existence is made up of the sum total of qualities that we strip from ourselves and project into an imaginary being distinct from ourselves.[7] "The impoverishment of the real world and the enriching of God is one act. Only the poor man has a rich God. God springs out of the feeling of a want."[8]

But we are quite willing, says Feuerbach, to diminish ourselves and immerse oursleves in this impoverishment. Why?

Because in our image of God we rediscover our own qualities elevated to the level of the unlimited infinite: "Our positive, essential qualities, our realities, are therefore the realities of God, but in us they exist with, in God without, limits."[9] In the last analysis "God is the highest subjectivity of man abstracted from himself."[10]

Thus to think, desire, and love is to be God. What exists outside our mind constitutes the world; what exists inside the mind, the capacity to reason and use the mind, is God.[11] Loving, in particular, means being God. Love makes a human being God, and God a human being. It is the activity that unifies God and human beings, spirit and nature. Apart from love, indeed, there is no God. God's love for us, the keystone of Christianity, is our love for ourselves objectified. Thus "God is for man the commonplace book where he registers his highest feelings and thoughts, the genealogical tree on which are entered the names that are dearest and most sacred to him."[12]

Having affirmed the illusory character of religion, Feuerbach goes back over all the main principles and dogmas of Christianity to show that they are mere projections of human nature. They are desires fleshed out by the human heart, for the essence of Christianity is the essence of human feeling and affectivity.[13] When we look at our awareness of self as a whole, for example, we find ourselves confronted with the doctrine of the Trinity: "God the Father is *I*, God the Son *Thou*. The *I* is understanding, the *Thou* love. . . . The Third Person in the Trinity expresses nothing further than the love of the two divine Persons towards each other; it is the unity of the Son and the Father, the idea of community, strangely enough regarded in its turn as a special personal being."[14] Our feelings of absence and loneliness almost call for a God who is a societal union of beings who love each other fervently.

What, then, is faith? Is it not simply "the infinite self-certainty of man, the undoubting certainty that his own subjective being is the objective, absolute being, the being of beings"?[15] By the same token Christ's resurrection satisfies our desire to obtain direct here-and-now certainty of our personal existence after death.

For our purposes here I don't think we need consider

Feuerbach's discussion and explanation of every Christian doctrine. The basic outline is clear enough. He starts from the gratuitous assumption that God does not objectively exist and that religion is illusory. From that starting point Feuerbach was able to show that there is a subjective explanation for all Christian principles and dogmas. But what remains of his theory if in reality God does exist? Feuerbach never even attempted to raise that question. He simply started off from the assumption that God does not exist.

In *The Essence of Christianity* we also find hints of the various theories about the origin of religion that would later echo through Marxian thought and Marx's own critique of Hegel's philosophy. Thus we hear from Feuerbach that "this open-air of the heart, this outspoken secret, this uttered sorrow of the soul, is God. God is a tear of love, shed in the deepest concealment over human misery. 'God is an unutterable sigh, lying in the depths of the heart' (Sebastian Frank von Wörd): this saying is the most remarkable, the profoundest, truest expression of Christian mysticism."[16]

The origin of religion is rooted in two sources, according to Feuerbach. One is the intellect, the other is the emotions. On the one hand individuals find it impossible to attribute to themselves the various human qualities in a process of continuing growth and perfectionism; so the tendency is to picture these qualities as unlimited perfections and to attribute them to some other "being" who is distinct from self and lives in another world. We surrender, offering our perfected qualities to an idealized, illusory being who is the object of our fantasies and projections. On the other hand we also create religion out of an emotional matrix. Unable to find surcease from the sadness of life, we escape into an imaginary paradise. Faced with the harshness of social and political realities, we begin to cherish the desire for a better life after death.[17]

Once we have rejected God, it is only natural that we ourselves should occupy God's place and that theology should become a sublimated anthropology. This liberative and humanistic anthropology restores to us all that was best in us, all that we had stripped away from ourselves and accumulated to form the idea of God. Henceforth we are to be our own God. As was the case with Nietzsche, Feuerbach's atheism makes sense only if we use the death of God to inaugurate a life that is more and more humane. Henceforth human beings should live lives of mutual love and understanding, based on their newfound divinity. They do not need some alien being to guarantee or demand love: "Love for man must be no derivative love; it must be original. If human nature is that highest nature to man, then practically also the highest and first law must be the love of man for man. *Homo homini Deus est*: this is the great practical principle, . . . the axis on which revolves the history of the world."[18]

De Lubac has called Feuerbach the "spiritual father" of Marxist atheism and its greatest theologian.[19] Feuerbach certainly did offer an acute critique of religion and Christianity, thereby divinizing humanity in the process and profoundly affecting the later elaboration of Marxist atheism. In fact Marx himself did start from Feuerbach's ideas, as we shall see later, only to inject much more social content into them. Despite its sharp edge, however, Feuerbach's philosophy does not tackle certain essential questions. It avoids the whole root problem of the origin of being and the ultimate explanation of given reality. It starts off from the gratuitous assumption that God does not exist, and so the whole framework suffers from the gratuitousness of its base. It proposes to offer us an explanation of religious life and being, but it fails to explore the ultimate roots of not only religious being but being itself. To paraphrase Heidegger, it does not deal with "the being of being." Its key for explaining all religious phenomena is humanity, but it disregards the fact that humanity itself is a radical question more than an answer to anything.

We might agree with Feuerbach that philosophy alone does not suffice to prove the existence of God. (Neither does it suffice to deny God's existence.) But he ignores the fact that God himself has responded to the question as to who or what we are. God's response demands the best and the fullest from us, demands all that Feuerbach wanted to see us do according to what he had to say in the Heidelberg lectures I quoted earlier. Feuerbach used his rejection of God as the spring-board for the divinization of humanity; but he ignored the fact that Christianity proclaims the radical immediacy of God's presence in every human being. We do not have to impoverish ourselves in order to enrich some abstract conception of God. On the contrary, it was God who impoverished himself and shared our human frailities in order to allow us to be divinized.

With Christ, God reveals himself to us in the radical immediacy of each human being. Love for others in Christianity is not secondary or derivative, as Feuerbach thought. It does not tell us that we should love our neighbor because God commands us to do so rather than for our neighbor's own sake; nor does it say that we are to love God in people without ever really loving human beings themselves. Quite the contrary is the case. The love demanded of the Christian is radically original. Only by loving others, each and every human being, can the Christian love God. It is not that we are supposed to love God in human beings. It is that we can love God only by loving them. The distinctively Christian commandment is not so much the commandment to love God as the commandment to love human beings. We love God only by loving human beings.

Sigmund Freud

In *The Freudian Left* Paul Robinson tells us that Sigmund Freud saw himself more as an explorer than as a scientist. At the end of his life he sometimes compared his intellectual adventure with the religious mission of Moses. He did for the twentieth century what Marx had done for the nineteenth century.[20] Paul Ricoeur regards psychoanalysis as a new way of interpreting culture and humanity.[21] There can be no doubt, in any case, about a few points. Freud is one of the most solid pillars of contemporary culture. Insofar as our subject is concerned, it is clear that his psychology, fashioned in the interests of authentic, liberative humanism, had a devastating effect on the concept of God and religious principles.

Freud was certainly one of the most convinced and radical atheists in our modern culture. That can readily be seen by anyone who leafs through *The Future of an Illusion, Civilization and Its Discontents,* and *Moses and Monotheism.* Ernest Jones, his biographer, depicts him as a born atheist from one end of his life to the other. Freud never saw any reason to believe in the existence of a supernatural being; nor did he ever feel an emotional need to entertain such a belief. To him, as to Feuerbach, religion seemed to be merely an illusion that had to be replaced by a rigorously scientific way of thinking. In *The Future of an Illusion* he insists that science is not an illusion. What would be illusory would be to assume that we can look elsewhere for something that science cannot give us.

At this point, however, I must point out that illusion is not exactly the same thing as error in Freud's mind. Or, to put it another way, it is not necessarily an error. On rare occasions an illusion may be turned into a reality, though normally there is no solid reason to expect that it will be. It is something like the golden dream of a servant girl, says Freud, who imagines that some prince will come along, fall madly in love with her, and carry her off with him. It is not absolutely impossible for that to happen, but it is highly unlikely. A belief, then, is called an illusion by Freud when the person's desire to see it fulfilled is an important factor in its formulation. "It would be quite extraordinary if there were a God who created the world, a loving providence, a moral order in the universe, and another life beyond this one. It would be quite surprising if all that proved to be exactly as we wish it to be. And it would be even more astounding if our knavish and ignorant ancestors had managed to solve all these problematic issues about the universe."[22]

According to Freud, the origin of religion lies in our impotence vis-à-vis the external forces of nature and the instinctive forces within ourselves. We can hardly imagine how primitive people could have successfully confronted the terrors of life without the comfort offered by the illusion of religion. Thus religion arose at the early, primitive stage of human development. People were not yet able to use their reason to confront the forces of nature and their own instinctive drives. They either had to repress them or to face up to them with the help of other affective forces. Confronted with these dangerous and uncontrollable forces, people went back to their earlier experience and recalled their childhood. They remembered how protected they felt by their fathers, to whom they attributed superior wisdom and power. They were assured of love and protection by those fathers so long as they obeyed and avoided transgressing orders.[23] At the end of his study of Leonardo da Vinci, Freud sums up his view succinctly: "Psychoanalysis has made us cognizant of the intimate connection between the father-complex and faith in God. It has taught us that the personal God is simply an exalted father in psychological terms. Everyday experience indicates that young people readily tend to lose their religious faith when the authority of the father fades." Freud states the same view in *Totem and Taboo,* using almost the exact same language.[24]

In short, then, nostalgia for the father lies at the origin of our ideas about religion, and this nostalgia ultimately derives from the Oedipus complex. Since the Oedipus complex is viewed as universal by Freud, he can conclude that "religion is the universal obsessional neurosis of humanity, just as the obsessional neuroses of children derive from the Oedipus complex, from their relationship to their parents."[25]

In *Totem and Taboo* Freud attempts to explain the origin of all these neuroses. In the primitive horde, he explains, the father kept all the women for himself and prevented his sons from having any sexual contact with them. One day the sons got together, killed their father and devoured him, and thus put an end to the patriarchal horde.

United they had the courage to do something that they could not have carried out on their own as individuals. . . . Being savage cannibals, they would naturally devour their victim after killing him. The violent father had undoubtedly been the model feared and envied by each of the sons. By devouring him they attained identification with him and acquired something of his power. The totemic meal, which may be the most ancient human festival, would be the repetition and commemoration of the memorable (and criminal) event that gave rise to so many things: e.g., social and community organization, moral restrictions, and religion.[26]

On this basis Freud attempts to show that all religion is an attempt to resolve the guilt feelings that arose from the murder of the primitive father. The parricides satisfied their hatred by murdering the father and their desires by identifying with him. Then their repressed feelings of tenderness set in once again, taking the form of remorse. Thus arose the feeling of guilt, which coincides with the remorse that we all feel. The murdered father suddenly became stronger and even more important than he had been when alive. The sons "undid their own action by declaring that it was illicit to slay the father substitute, the totem; and they renounced the fruits of their action by denying themselves all sexual contact with the women who had been liberated. Thus out of their own feelings of guilt they created the two fundamental taboos of totemism; and for the very same reason those taboos must be closely linked up with the two repressed desires of the Oedipus complex."[27]

With the passage of time, the feeling of guilt and the expiation would give rise to an overwhelming nostalgia for the father. This in turn would easily give rise to the idea of an ideal father. Once divinized, the ideal father provided a readier means of reconciliation than the former relationship to the totem. The primitive father, who had been assassinated, was elevated to a God from which the clan claimed descent. This, according to Freud, was a much more serious effort at expiation than the old covenant with the totem had been.[28]

In Freud's eyes, satisfaction and sacrifice offered to God obviously are reconciliatory and expiatory; they are attempts to wipe away the primitive feeling of guilt described above. In a later stage of development, the animal involved lost its sacred character and sacrifice was reduced to the offering of gifts designed to appease the deity and gain his good will. Eventually the deity was elevated so high that a corps of priests had to be instituted to serve as intermediaries between God and human beings. At the same time, however, the increasing distance from God caused the feeling of guilt to pale into something vague and unconscious. The desire of the son to occupy the place of God the Father intensified. Christ offered himself up voluntarily, becoming God in the place of the father. One sign of this change was the revival of the ancient ritual and the totemic meal in the form of communion. Instead of devouring the father, however, the brothers would eat the flesh and drink the blood of the son. Thus Freud concludes that there is a link between all these things: the totemic feast, animal sacrifice, the theanthropic sacrifice, and the Christian eucharist. All of them are the result of a crime that weighed heavily on human beings but of which they also had to feel proud. At bottom Christian communion is "a repetition of the crime that had to be expiated. Thus Frazer is quite justified . . . when he tells us that Christian communion is an adaptation of a sacrament much older than Christianity."[29]

For Freud, then, religion is ultimately nothing more than an illusion. Its origin lies in the Oedipus complex, which in turn arose from the murder of the primitive father at the dawn of history. It is there we must look for the beginnings of religion, morality, society, and art. And this corresponds perfectly with the findings of psychoanalysis, which show that the Oedipus complex is at the core of all neuroses.[30] Our yearning for the father goes hand in hand with our need to be protected against the consquences of our human frailty. It is the child's reaction against feelings of impotence that furnishes the main traits for the adult's reaction against the impotence that must be accepted. And it is precisely this reaction "that gives rise to religion."[31]

In the last analysis, then, the fact of religion is interpreted genetically in terms of the unconscious. As far as Freud could see, that pretty well exhausted the content and the significance of religion. No objective reality lay behind it at all.

Freud's feeling was that chaos would reign once humanity fully realized that religion was an illusion. Humankind would feel naked and defenseless once deprived of the illusory convictions that had provided us with so much consolation and security throughout past history. Yet the realization itself was inevitable, for the progress of science and scholarship could not help but uncover the true bases of faith and thereby undermine it. To avoid chaos, culture and morality would have to be gradually stripped of their religious underpinnings and rooted more and more solidly in reason and the sciences.

Thus to reject religion is to foster a culture and a morality devoid of illusions; it is to pave the way for a truly liberated life. Freud, then, is following in the footsteps of Nietzsche and Feuerbach. His reduction of religion to mere illusion is merely the reverse side of a basically positive attitude that seeks to liberate people and help them to be more authentically human. Freud wants us to regain the power that we have lost by transferring it to some remote, imaginary transcendence. As Paul Ricoeur puts it:

Whether it is a question of the Marxist leap from the realm of necessity into that of liberty by means of scientific understanding of the laws of history, or of the Nietzschean contemplation of destiny and eternal recurrence, or, in Freud's language, of the passage from the pleasure principle to the reality principle, it is always the same undertaking: to reveal man to himself, in his power of affirmation and creation of meaning. . . . Freud . . . has not only, or even principally, introduced a new kind of therapy, but a global interpretation of the phenomenon of culture and of religion as an aspect of culture.[32]

Freud viewed psychoanalysis as a weapon that would free us from our religious illusions and fantasies. But it should be obvious that psychoanalysis, like any scientific method, ought to adopt an attitude of neutrality toward the alternatives of theism and atheism. Indeed Freud himself admitted this in a letter which he wrote to O. Pfister, the Protestant minister who was one of the first to show an interest in the pastoral uses of psychoanalysis: "Taken in itself, psychoanalysis is neither religious nor antireligious. It is an impartial instrument which can serve both clergy and lay people as a means to help people who are suffering. It has astounded me to realize that it has taken me so long to appreciate . . . the extraordinary contribution which the psychoanalytic method might make to pastoral work."

But while Freud might acknowledge the religious neutrality of psychoanalysis in principle, his own principles and convictions would affect his own use of it. In his hands psychoanalysis became a powerful weapon aimed against every religious idea. He saw religion as a universal obsessional neurosis and God as an exalted Father.[33]

I am not going to go into a detailed critique of Freudian principles here. That is a task for professional psychologists. But I would like to point out that in Freud's line of reasoning we find many gaps, discontinuities, unproved hypotheses, and bold extrapolations. Freud himself was aware of this, and he compared himself to a ballerina balancing on the tips of her toes.[34] He even came to admit that religion was on a scale of grandeur that eluded the reach of his reasoning power.[35]

Nevertheless Freud did transform psychoanalysis into a tool for explaining religion fully. Convinced of the nonexistence of God, he forced his scientific theories to prove the view that he had adopted from the very start. Now we know that no scientific method can really prove or disprove the existence of God. Freud himself realized that, but he disregarded it in practice. To that extent he went against the aim of scientific fidelity that he had set for himself and God are just that: theories and interesting lucubrations. The problem is that there is a fatal flaw in their very starting point.

Moreover, Freud's theories have been amply discussed and debated by his own disciples and successors. In many instances they have been revised or simply superseded. The universality of the Oedipus complex is not accepted by many, including Adler, Horney, Harry Stack Sullivan, and Jung. Malinowski wondered why the Oedipus complex and its consequences would not disappear with the passage of time. Jung maintained that the Oedipal tendency was not a desire for intimate physical union with the father. And going directly against Freud's view, he maintained that religion is a basic factor in integral emotional adjustment. Essential to any effective therapy, he said, is a religion that is intellectually and emotionally satisfying. For him religion is "a careful and scrupulous observation of what Rudolf Otto termed the *numinosum,* that is, a dynamic agency or effect not caused by an arbitrary act of will. On the contrary, it seizes and controls the human subject, who is always rather its victim than its creator."[36]

According to Jung, we do not come to know God as a theological concept but rather as a primary experience; from this we then go on to formulate certain theological concepts. Jung even goes so far as to view the unconscious as essentially religious. He tells us that all religions have their psychological roots in the collective unconscious of the race. Hence the influence of the unconscious on us is basically a religious phenomenon.[37] For Freud religion is a universal obsessional neurosis. For Jung the absence of religion is one of the chief causes of psychological disorders in adults.

It should be apparent that I am not citing Jung here because I think his explanation is correct. It is subject to the same criticism as that directed against Freud's theory insofar as any attempt to reduce God or religion to scientific explanations is doomed to failure. I cited Jung here to show that people can use the same scientific rigor to arrive at very opposite conclusions, depending on the principles or goals they have set for themselves at the start (not as scientists but as human beings).

Insofar as Freud's ideas about totemism are concerned, they have been widely criticized. Some deny that totemism is a universal practice, and others maintain that it does not necessarily belong to any primitive stage of human development. Religion is viewed as positive for human development by many important psychologists: e.g., Gordon Allport. Today we even find atheists (e.g., Fromm and Huxley) trying to promote a humanist religion that will enable people to escape from the suffocating atmosphere of superficial living, emptiness, and scientism. Finally, it is worth noting W.H. Biddle's remark about the idea of God: The fact that the child entertains the idea of an omnipotent father does not ipso facto make the idea of God infantile or imaginary as Freud gratuitously assumed.

I don't think we need go into more detailed criticisms of Freud's doctrine, for that goes beyond the bounds of our present chapter.[38] The point I wish to make here has to do with Freud's atheism. While it was dogmatic and devastating and devoid of solid grounding, it aimed in the last analysis to foster human liberation. In Freud's hands psychoanalysis sought to liberate us by showing that religion is an illusion bound up with our desire; it sought to destroy the God that we had fabricated for ourselves.

The only problem is that these conclusions are already present in Freud's point of departure, and his point of departure is a wholly gratuitous one. Once he assumes that God does not exist, then he must offer some psychological explanation for the idea of God and its origin. But as we have noted above, God transcends all observation and science; no science can say anything valid about God as such. Taking a somewhat different route, Freud arrived at conclusions similar to those of Feuerbach. The reason is that both started out with the same presuppositions and the same goal: to free humanity. They simply never imagined that God could have manifested himself to us as our Liberator.

Bertrand Russell

A major philosopher, mathematician, and humanist, Bertrand Russell stands out among the many thinkers who have continued to regard God as an illusion. His philosophy, which seeks to be profoundly humanitarian, is basically antireligious.

Russell was a neo-realist in the tradition of empirical realism that goes back to Hume. In his view only the methods of the natural sciences can provide us with valid knowledge. Any truth supposedly obtained from some other source must be rejected as illusory. Even philosophy itself must be essentially scientific if it wants to retain its claim to validity. In posing its problems it must base itself on the natural sciences, not on such things as religion or morality. All "romanticism" and "mysticism" must be excluded. Only the natural sciences can provide us with valid information about reality, and we must rest content with the realization that we can never get beyond some sort of probabilism. (In the latter point Russell is reminiscent of Reichenbach.)

His sharpest criticisms were always directed against such notions as interiority, personality, subjectivism, the soul, and God. Such subjective "nonsense" is indefensible. Such illusory language is dangerous because it induces us to live in a world of fantasies. The natural sciences are the only source of information and knowledge, and they provide no basis at all for faith in God, the soul, immortality, and the like.

Russell believed that religion was rooted in fear, that it was therefore an evil from which humanity had to be freed. It was also an enemy of decency and goodness in the modern world, bearing witness to human beings who had not yet come of age. The notion of the "person" as enduring and stable was too closely bound up with the idea of substance to be given serious consideration. In that respect he would probably agree with A.J. Ayer that the person is simply a logical construct.

Thus the philosophy of Russell—but not his ethics—begins with the idea of the human being as a nonentity. A close look reveals a big nothing at the heart of this nonentity. We are a series of fleeting, momentary experiences, an experiment leading toward nothingness.

In *A Free Man's Worship* Russell maintains that everything is a product of chance. Everything ends up in absolute nothingness. It is only in thinking that we are really free, "free from our fellowmen, free from the petty planet on which our bodies impotently crawl, free even, while we live, from the tyranny of death." We must simply try to face the situation with courage: "To defy with Promethean constancy a hostile universe, to keep its evil always in view, always actively hated, to refuse no pain that the malice of Power can invent, appears to be the duty of all who will not bow before the inevitable." If we want to live, then we must build our foundation on courageous despair:

That Man is the product of causes which had no prevision of the end they were achieving: that his origin, his growth, his hopes and fears, his loves and beliefs, are but the outcome of accidental collocations of atoms; that no fire, no heroism, no intensity of thought and feeling, can preserve an individual life beyond the grave; that all the labour of the ages, all the devotion, all the inspiration, all the noonday brightness of human genius, are destined to extinction in the vast death of the solar system, and that the whole temple of Man's achievement must inevitably be buried beneath the debris of a universe in ruins—all these things, if not quite beyond dispute, are yet so nearly certain, that no philosophy which rejects them can hope to stand.

Only within the scaffolding of these truths, only on the firm foundation of unyielding despair, can the soul's habitation henceforth be
safely built.[39]

   In his ethics Bertrand Russell was a radical humanist, opposing every type of injustice, oppression, and war. The only real
principle of his morality seemed to be "the good life," that is, a
life motivated by practical love and guided by the help of
knowledge. He acknowledges that rules and norms for practical ethics are inevitable, but he also insists that the existing ones
must be changed insofar as they rest on superstitious beliefs.
This is evident in the whole area of sexual morality (including
monogamy) and in such practices as war, the death penalty,
and the use of torture. The ideal of individual salvation, being
an aristocratic ideal, should be eradicated because it runs
counter to the ideal of societal salvation; the latter is much
more in line with democracy. The ideal of individual salvation,
by contrast, promotes excessive individualism and personal
isolation, which are inimical to social integration.
   What matters to Russell, then, is the way humanity goes
about seeking and obtaining its goal. The attainment of that
goal must be open to all, not just to a few as it has been so far.
Humanity must be liberated from all fear and anxiety, learn-
ing to dominate life completely with the help of science.
   Russell was always a pacifist, from the days of World War I
when he was imprisoned for his pacifism to his last years when
he was protesting against the Vietnam war. He seems to be the
perfect example of the atheistic humanist who is deeply concerned for the welfare of humanity but who sees the idea of
God as an illusion that poses an obstacle to full human development. Such an illusion must be rejected. Like Feuerbach
and Freud, Russell wants us to become free by abandoning our
silly notions.
   A profoundly humanistic impulse guided the three men
whom we have considered in this chapter. They rejected God
as an illusory idea without any scientific basis. They had no
knowledge of, or no particular desire to accept, a God who had
revealed himself in a succession of liberating events and who

himself had become our liberation—though he never had or would reveal himself in the experiments of science. God as illusion certainly should be rejected, for God is not an illusion. God is the Word who has spoken to us and the world, and who has incarnated himself in the real course of liberation.

Notes

1. Many of my comments here on Feuerbach are taken from my previous work, *La revolución con Marx y con Cristo* (Caracas: Monte Avila, 1973).

2. See Karl Barth's "Introductory Essay" to *The Essence of Christianity*, Eng. trans. (New York: Harper & Row, 1957).

3. Ibid., p. xvi.

4. Walter H. Capps regards *The Essence of Christianity* as the "still-most-threatening-of-all-critiques of religion" (*Cross Currents* 18 [1968]: 264). It is certain that Feuerbach's critique of Christianity and religion would prove to have a devastating effect. Marx and Engels applauded it, and thus it found its way into the core of Marxist atheism.

5. L. Feuerbach, *The Essence of Christianity*, p. xxxvi.

6. Ibid., pp. 12–14.

7. Ibid., p. 26.

8. Ibid., p. 73.

9. Ibid., p. 38.

10. Ibid., p. 31.

11. Ibid., p. 40.

12. Ibid., pp. 63–64.

13. Ibid., p. 140.

14. Ibid., p. 67.

15. Ibid., p. 127.

16. Ibid., p. 122.

17. Ibid., p. 136.

18. Ibid., p. 271.

19. Henri de Lubac, *The Drama of Atheist Humanism*, Eng. trans. (Cleveland: Meridian Books, 1963), p. 14.

20. See Paul A. Robinson, *The Freudian Left* (New York: Harper & Row, 1969), pp. 2 and 7.

21. See Paul Ricoeur, *Freud and Philosophy: An Essay on Interpretation*, Eng. trans. (New Haven: Yale University Press, 1970).

22. Sigmund Freud, *The Future of an Illusion* (Garden City, N.Y.: Doubleday Anchor, 1964), pp. 49, 52–53. The works of Freud are available in various English translations.

23. See Erich Fromm, *Psychoanalysis and Religion* (New Haven: Yale University Press, 1950), p. 11.

24. Sigmund Freud, *Totem and Taboo* (New York: Norton, 1950), p. 147.

25. Sigmund Freud, *The Future of an Illusion*, pp. 70–71.

26. Freud, *Totem and Taboo*, p. 128.

27. Ibid.

28. Ibid., p. 149.

29. Ibid., p. 208.

30. S. Freud, *The Future of an Illusion*, p. 35.

31. Ibid., p. 66f.

32. Paul Ricoeur, "The Atheism of Freudian Psychoanalysis," in *Concilium* 16 (New York: Paulist Press, 1966), pp. 60–61.

33. Most of the psychoanalysts of the first generation adopted or held Freud's conviction that psychoanalysis would eventually replace religion, and that psychoanalysis would assume the role of pastors of souls that had been reserved for priests in older cultures. O. Pfister and Lou Andreas Salomé, the latter a pupil of Freud, were notable exceptions to this trend.

34. S. Freud, *Gesammelte Werke* (London: Imago, 1941), 16:160.

35. Ibid., p. 236. This and the preceding quote are taken from the anthology entitled *El ateismo contemporáneo* (Madrid: Ed. Cristiandad, 1971), p. 261.

36. K. Jung, *Psychology and Religion* (New Haven: Yale University Press, 1938).

37. Ibid., p. 46.

38. Still valid and interesting material can be found in the critiques of Dalbiez and Maritain. See Roland Dalbiez, *Psychoanalytical Method and the Doctrine of Freud*, Eng. trans., 2 vols. (London: Longmans, Green & Co., 1947); and Jacques Maritain, *Quatre essais sur l'Esprit dans sa condition charnelle* (Paris: Alsatia, 1956).

39. Bertrand Russell, *A Free Man's Worship* (London: Penguin Books, Pelican, 1953), p. 51.

9

GOD AS AN OBSTACLE TO THE LIBERATION OF THE OPPRESSED: MARX

Heaven was invented to satisfy those human beings to whom the earth offers nothing.
—Heine (a friend of Marx)

The abolition of religion as the illusory happiness of human beings is required for their real-life happiness. The summons to give up the illusions of their condition is a summons to give up a condition that requires illusions. . . . Thus criticism of heaven is converted into criticism of the earth, criticism of religion into criticism of law, and criticism of theology into criticism of politics.
—Karl Marx

It seems to be a well established fact that Marx opted for atheism at a relatively early age.[1] Contrary to what some of his biographers once maintained, he does not seem to have gone through any religious crisis in his youth; nor did he ever show any real sympathy toward believers.[2] There was no period of religiosity, as there was in the case of many of the young Hegelians: e.g., Feuerbach, Bruno Bauer, and Engels.

Engels, for example, prayed every day at the age of nine-

151

teen. He "wept copious tears" trying to find his way back to the faith of his childhood. As for Feuerbach, he himself declared that "God was my first thought, reason my second, and man my third and final one." In his case we have already seen how his acquaintance with Hegelianism and his conviction that the existence of God could not be proved rationally changed his life. Instead of becoming a Protestant minister, he opted for atheism.

Marx, on the other hand, never seems to have attached any importance to faith. This seems to come across clearly even in his doctoral dissertation (1841), which dealt with differences between the natural philosophy of Democritus and that of Epicurus. He praised Epicurus as the greatest philosopher of the Greek Enlightenment because he had "replaced the old idols with the new divinity of man." Marx's words seem to echo those of Lucretius in *De Rerum Natura* on Epicurus. Lucretius praised him for being "the first mortal who dared to challenge the gods in heaven, who dared to free humanity from the oppressive weight of religion, . . . who dared to look the gods firmly in the face and challenge them."[3] One of the principles of Epicurus was that "the ultimate aim of pleasure is to live as a god among men." In it we can easily find one of the remote roots of Marx's own philosophical structure, for Marx sought to restore to humanity its lost divinity.

From a very early age Marx came to feel that the full realization and exaltation of humanity called for the total rejection of God and religion. As he wrote to Hardmann years later: "The religion of the workers has no god because it seeks to restore the divinity to man."[4]

The young Marx was fascinated by another figure even more than he was impressed by Epicurus. Like Fichte and Goethe before him, Marx was fascinated by the figure of Prometheus, the father of technology. Prometheus stole fire from the gods and tried to make man like God. As punishment for his rebellion against Jupiter, he was chained to a cliff and subjected to torture; but he never asked for mercy. The fact is that Marx never really went into the question of God's existence or nonexistence. His response might well have been that of Prometheus to Hermes, the messenger from Jupiter: "I will never change my lot for enslavement. I prefer to be chained to a cliff than to be the slave of Jupiter."[5] In his doctoral dissertation Marx wrote: "Philosophy cannot keep its secret any longer. Prometheus' profession of faith is its own: I hate all gods. Philosophy maintains this attitude against all the earthly and celestial gods who refuse to recognize human consciousness as the supreme deity."[6]

Since Marx was essentially a revolutionary, his own doctrine is dominated by the idea of praxis. Ideas are legitimate only if they lead to liberative action. And since faith in God must be eradicated if human revolution and liberation are to be successful, human beings must be helped to give up their faith in God's existence. Thus Marxist atheism is not really a philosophic conclusion; instead it is the speculative justification of a politico-practical decision. Marx proceeds to prove that God has existed as an illusion in people's minds only after he had already decided to do away with God.

The position of Marx, and of Engels, found support in the skirmishes of the young Hegelians: e.g., Bruno Bauer, Arnold Ruge, and Max Stirner. But several other works would eventually lay the antireligious and antitheistic formulation of Marxist thinking. Strauss's *Life of Jesus* appeared in 1835. In it the author maintained that the gospel accounts were myths, pure legends created and supernaturalized by the disciples of Jesus. In 1841 Feuerbach's book *The Essence of Christianity* appeared, and in 1851 his book *The Essence of Religion*. In *The German Ideology* Marx and Engels wrote:

Up to now human beings have held false conceptions about their own being and their future. They have structured their relations on the basis of their ideas about God and man. Thus they have capitulated to the fantasies of their own brains. They, the creators, have bowed and bent their knees before their creatures. Hence it is our duty to free them from the chimeras, ideas, dogmas, and imaginary beings under whose yoke they now move. It is our duty to revolutionize them against the dictates of their imagination. One (Feuerbach) says: Let us teach them to trade in their imaginings for ideas that correspond with the essence of man. Another (Bruno Bauer) says: Let us teach them to take a critical attitude toward them. Still another (Max Stirner) wants these imaginings to be expelled from men's minds once and for all. In this way the false reality now in existence will collapse completely.[7]

In this criticism of religion, Marx starts from Feuerbach: "The basis of religious criticism is simply this—it is man who makes religion, not religion that makes man."[8] As we have already seen, Feuerbach began with the premise that God is merely an illusion, a projection of the various qualities of human nature. The affirmations of religion are projections of human individuals, extrojecting their ideal picture of themselves on to an imaginary being. Marx would start off from Feuerbach's conception, but he would stress the social dimension:

In fact religion is simply the awareness that man has of himself. However, man is not an abstract being wandering outside this world. Man is the human world, the state, society. It is the state and society that produces religion. Religion is the inversion of the conceptual world precisely because this world is in fact inverted.[9]

For this reason the rational critique of religion must become a practical critique of the socio-political conditions that produce and maintain religious awareness and the religious outlook. In the last analysis Feuerbach never clearly explained why it is that human beings keep projecting their own ideas into another world. In Marx's eyes, Feuerbach failed to give due weight to the social conditions that are at the root of religious projections. He did not give due emphasis to praxis. Instead he spoke of man as an abstract being.

For Marx it is work that turns a being into a human being; through it human beings conquer nature. They differentiated themselves from brute animals and became human beings insofar as they began to produce objects. And the shared experience of work created solidarity between human beings as well as societal history. The bonds of union between human beings and the march of social history are not secured by any "religious or political nonsense."[10] They are secured by the continuity of the means of production.

With the introduction of the means of production, there arose a distinction between human beings. Human beings were divided into owners and servants, social classes were created, and a threefold alienation—sociological, ideological, and religious—was spawned in the proletariat. We now find ourselves alienated, divided from ourselves within and unable to fulfill ourselves as human beings in our work. We are forced to sell our labor, but we cannot acquire the fruits of it for ourselves. The product of our labor only enhances the power of those who own the means of production. In present-day society workers are paid salaries; they are not the owners of the products of their work. So instead of helping them to attain human fulfillment and realize themselves creatively, work alienates and dehumanizes them:

The object produced by labor . . . stands over against man as an alien being, as an independent power. . . . The worker puts his life into the object. His life now belongs to that object rather than to himself. The more burdensome his activity, the less he possesses. That which is incorporated into the product of his labor is no longer his own. The greater his production, the more he himself is diminished. The alienation of the worker in the product of his work means not only that his work is turned into an object and takes on an external existence but also that it exists independently of himself. It stands over against him as something alien, opposing him as an autonomous power. The life which he has invested in the object turns against him, becoming an alien and hostile force.[11]

Thus in capitalism labor is external to the workers. It is imposed on them as "forced labor." Instead of fulfilling themselves in their work, the workers negate themselves. Instead of investing their mental and psychic energy in something that they like to do, they must invest it in something that they are forced to do. They sell their activity, their labor, to others in order to ensure their own subsistence. Their work is no longer the satisfaction of a need; it is only the means to satisfy other needs. So we come to this result: "Man (the laborer) feels that he is acting freely only in carrying out his animal functions (e.g., eating, drinking, and procreating) . . . while in his human functions he finds himself reduced to an animal. The animal side of him is turned into the human, and vice-versa."[12]

Moreover, the social and solidary nature of work is lost in capitalism. The workers are alienated from their fellows. They now come to be seen as competitors because the success of one is achieved at the expense of another. Individuals are closed up in themselves; their work companions are viewed solely as their own adversaries. One person is pitted against another, and human relationships take on an antagonistic character. Work had been the means whereby human beings achieved solidarity and community; now it becomes a means of frustrating those aims.

We are also alienated ideologically. The ideologies of state, philosophy, and religion are means whereby the owners and oppressors maintain their own positions. The state proclaims liberty, equality, and respect for all its citizens; but in fact it is only the organized collective power of landowners, capitalists, and the wealthy directed against the exploited laborers and peasants. Philosophical ideologies are likewise sellouts to those in power; their systematized formulations and conclusions merely help to maintain the situation of inequality and oppression.

A necessary consequence of social alienation is religious alienation. We imagine another world of fulfillment precisely because we find ourselves alienated in the world of work and can find no self-satisfaction. Hence religion is merely an epiphenomenon of social life. We escape to an illusory world because we cannot find security and happiness in the present world. As Heine put it: "Heaven was invented to satisfy those human beings to whom the earth offers nothing." Religion is needed insofar as it offers people consolation in an unjust and oppressive world, insofar as it justifies the concrete life of the oppressed and makes it bearable. Without the consolation of religion, life would be intolerable and progress would stagnate. That is why religion wells up time and again from the inhuman conditions of life.

At the same time, however, religion is the better side of a bad situation. As Marx himself put it: "Religious suffering is at once an expression of concrete suffering and a protest against it. Religion is the yearning of the oppressed creature, the feeling of a heartless world, the soul of soulless living conditions. Religion is the opiate of the people."[13] It is the last phrase of this statement, of course, that has been engraved on people's minds and turned into a slogan. However it is not the most illuminating and important point of the passage. Let us consider the passage in greater detail.

First of all, religion is viewed as an expression of suffering in this world, as "the yearning of the oppressed creature." The same phrase was used by Feuerbach, and he alluded to the words of Sebastian Franck von Wörd: "God is the imperishable yearning that wells up from the depths of the heart." At the same time, however, religion is also a "protest" against this suffering. It is futile and ineffective in Marx's view because it turns our attention and concern away from this world and focuses our hopes on another world. But it is only after he has underlined the human yearning and protest embodied in religion that Marx goes on to call it the "opiate" of the people. Its narcotic effect lies in the fact that it teaches people to accept unhappiness here on earth by offering them promises of happiness in heaven. That is what Marx is implying when he calls religion "the soul of soulless living conditions." Religion helps to bring joy to people's spirits, but only in an imaginary way; it does not bring any perduring joy into the conditions of real life. The medicine it offers people cannot cure the sickness that afflicts people and society; it can only alleviate the pain. What we must do now is cure the illness; then, and only then, the pain-killing drug will no longer be needed at all. As Marx puts it:

The abolition of religion, insofar as it is the illusory happiness of human beings, is required for their real happiness. The call to abandon the illusions of their condition is a call to abandon a condition which requires illusions. Hence the criticism of religion is, in germ, the criticism of this vale of tears of which religion is the crown. . . . The immediate task of a philosophy in the service of history is to unmask human alienation in its secular form once it has been unmasked in its religious form. Thus criticism of heaven becomes criticism of the earth, criticism of religion becomes criticism of law, and criticism of theology becomes criticism of politics.[14]

We must eradicate exploitation and put an end to inhuman social conditions. Once this is done, according to Marx, poverty will disappear; and, along with it, religion will disappear insofar as it is both an expression of poverty and a protest against it.

When society takes possession of all the means of production and uses them intelligently, thereby freeing itself and all its members from the bondage that now prevails, . . . when man can not only propose but dispose of these things, it is then that the ultimate power which is reflected in religion will disappear also. And with it will disappear religious reflection itself, for the simple reason that it will no longer have anything on which to reflect.[15]

In Marx's doctrine, religious awareness results in practice from the fact that individuals still form a unity with the natural community, or that they live in the direct relationship of master and slave, or that they have not yet developed even the most minimal individual awareness. Marx suggests that the direct relationship of master and slave has been abolished in modern bourgeois society through the introduction of the notion of equal rights before the law (freedom of contract). At that turning point in history the old natural religions of the common people prove to be inadequate. Christianity, with its abstract worship of the human being, now proves to be the most suitable religion for maintaining the oppression of the common people. This is particularly true of its bourgeois forms such as Protestantism and deism. The individualism of Protestant piety corresponds perfectly with the individual mode of production and the isolation of the workers. Now the only bond of union between the workers is the production process itself.

Marx views Protestant individualism as the chief root of the "capitalist spirit," and it is hard to quarrel with that view. The social principles of Christianity greatly help to maintain the capitalist mentality because they affirm "that all the actions of the oppressors against the oppressed are a just punishment for original sin or else tests which the Lord, in his infinite wisdom, imposes on the redeemed." These principles "preach cowardice, self-deprecation, degradation, subjugation, and humility. In short, they preach all the qualities of the *canaille* [the rabble]. The proletariat, which does not wish to be regarded as *canaille*, has need of courage, self-awareness, pride, and independence even more than it has need of bread." It is the social principles of Christianity which "justified slavery in Antiquity, glorified servitude in the Middle Ages, and today are perfectly capable of defending the oppression of the proletariat even though it looks on them with pity."[16]

In *Das Kapital* Marx predicts that religion will be superseded through a transformation in the mode of production that will permit "intelligible" and "reasonable" human relationships. The proletariat will take over the means of production. History is moving closer to that moment, and hence to the denial of religion. It is a natural, inevitable process. The dispossessors will be dispossessed. Once private property has been abolished, freedom and equality will reign and real human history will begin. Every form of alienation will disappear, and people will be able to be authentically human. Brotherhood and peace will flourish on this earthly paradise, and we will live happily in a classless society. Even atheism will no longer make any sense, for atheism is the denial of God that allows us to affirm ourselves. Once we can affirm ourselves in real life, God will not even be mentioned.

For Marx, then, human society takes the place of God and his divine perfections. Humanity is its own creator. It will find fulfillment in the members of society that is perfectly human, in a totality whose individual members relate to each other lovingly. In theory at least, the utopia of Marxist society and its atheistic religion fulfill the most noble aspirations of any genuine humanism.

In the last analysis Marx's concern with the theme of religion must be framed within his concern for a more general and basic problem: emancipation from every alienation. Marx was a great humanist. He rejected God in order to liberate people.

As I pointed out above, however, Marx never even tried to prove the nonexistence of God. He proposed to put an end to God, to erase any ideas about God from people's minds. For Marx atheism was a postulate, a cultural presupposition. It is not so much that his philosophy is an atheistic one; rather, it presupposes atheism. In his eyes Christianity was the same as idealistic philosophy; both served to embody and represent the superstructures of an oppressive, capitalistic society.[17]

But who exactly was the God that Marx had in mind? It was the image of Jupiter, who chained Prometheus to a cliff when he tried to help man. It was a God opposed to liberation and the progress of this world, a God who simply went bail for the unjust and inhuman conditions of this world. Now if that were the only possible image of God, then we all would have to join Marx in opposing him. A God opposed to human grandeur should be rejected. But it should be more than clear by now that such a God is a mere idol. It is not the God presented by biblical and Christian revelation, the God who wishes to create human community and to liberate us.

Marx rose up in rebellion against an idol. On that point we are in total agreement with him and we must imitate his example. Marx rightly highlighted many degenerate aspects of Christianity and the church, pointing out basic flaws and failures; for that we should be grateful to him. Marx displayed intense and authentic humanism in placing himself on the side of the poor and the oppressed. In that respect he was much more Christian than Christians themselves, and we should do all we can to follow his example. Marx was the Good Samaritan of history. He stopped to heal the wounds of the wounded victim who had been bypassed by the priests, the economic planners, and the politicians.

It is clear that Marx touched the basic core of the Christian message and authentic religion, even with all his atheism. But we cannot agree that his idea of God is the only possible one. Every human being would and should rebel against the God Marx caricatured. But it would be a serious mistake not to go beyond Marx and realize that his God is not the only possible one. His own critical, scientific theory would lead us to go beyond him if it could be shown that religion is a leaven of liberation rather than an opiate, that God is not opposed to human liberation but is rather our supreme liberator.

It is certainly true that official Marxist dogma, as espoused by Russia and its allies, has done nothing more than mimic Marx's view of religion and God. But many other thinkers, particularly practicing Marxists, have gone far beyond Marx's view. On the level of practice we find more and more people involved in the process of liberation who do not even ask whether their companions are believers or not. They believe in humanity and dedicate themselves to humanity's cause. That is enough. Their lives embody the practical understanding that Palmiro Togliatti tried to urge upon Communists and Catholics years ago when he called upon both sides to unite for the basic aim of saving civilization and the world.[18] Starting from different conceptions, they seek to arrive at the same goal: human liberation. For some of them God is a superfluous entity; for others God is the motivating force and goal of their commitment. Both attack the improper use of God and the worship of an idol, some in the name of humanity and the nonexistence of God, others in the name of humanity and a liberator God. At the heart of their commitment lies a great act of faith: on the one hand faith in humankind for humankind's sake, on the other hand faith in humankind insofar as it is also faith in God.

On the theoretical level, Marxism today seems less and less to be a universal plan for life aimed directly *against* God. Instead it seems to offer the positive possibility of a fully liberated life for humanity *without* God.[19] We find more and more Marxist thinkers and politicians who have gotten beyond the conception of Christianity and God held by official, dogmatic Marxism. Among them we might well single out Ernst Bloch and Roger Garaudy as the most well known and influential among those who are open to the idea of dialogue between Marxists and Christians.

Along with Lukacs, Korsch, and others, *Ernst Bloch* seems to be the principal exponent of esoteric Marxism. This is a current within Marxism that seeks to go beyond the confines of Leninism and Stalinism and back to the pre-Marxist sources of prophetic history in Judaism and Christianity as well as to the politico-religious manifestations of revolutionary history in the West. The publication of Bloch's *Das Prinzip Hoffnung* ("The Hope Principle") marked a major moment in Christian-Marxist dialogue. It would have a profound influence on the theology of hope as elaborated by Metz, Alves, and Moltmann.

Bloch is a loner, a messianic and utopian thinker. He speaks for a revision of the Marxist tradition. Using Kantian categories, he tells us that Marxism is a critique of pure reason that still lacks its critique of practical reason. His aim is to contribute to the Marxist critique of practical reason, to get beyond the limits of dialectical materialism and give due weight to the eschatological dimension:

It can be said that the extraordinary emphasis on economics and the total neglect of all the factors of transcendence place Marxism in the realm of a critique of pure reason that has not yet been complemented and completed with a critique of practical reason. It talks much about economics, but it says nothing at all about the spirit and faith—which certainly deserve mention.[20]

For Bloch there is no reason why religion—along with fantasy, dreams, and mysticism—should be merely a cause of alienation. They are something essential to, and inherent in, the human essence. Religious awareness takes in human needs, motives, and "spheres" that are indeed bound up with socio-economic revolution but which certainly cannot be explained solely by it. Bloch thinks that there has been too much talk about economic life and not enough about human life. The meaning of humankind is not exhausted when we explore and explain it in socio-economic terms. Even after we have said all that can be said about socio-economic causes and conditions, human beings remain an open, unanswered question. We are a process, a *homo absconditus*. Like the world around us, we are both a task and "a gigantic receptacle fraught with the future." We are beings constantly straining forward toward our full realization.

One of the great merits of Bloch surely lies in the fact that he has gone back to champion the teleological character of Marxism, thereby reuniting it with the noblest and loftiest religious traditions. Bloch has served as a bridge between Christian teachings and Marxist doctrines by stressing the need for both to revitalize themselves. Neither can view itself as "firmly fixed and established." Both must continue to move toward their future, searching for a better humanism and more sincerely devoting themselves to the problem of concrete humanity.

It is true that Bloch sharply criticizes the institutionalized church. To him it is a "structure of compromises." It is always ready to adapt to "what is" instead of straining and struggling for "what is not yet." As an institution overly concerned with the "hereafter," it tends to persecute those prophets who want it to keep looking for a new heaven and a new earth. But Bloch is equally critical of static, dogmatic Marxism. For the latter, he says, robs us of our eschatological dimension and our capacity for religion.

In Bloch's thought Marxism ends up being the theory, the practice of which is religion. Both are independent but complementary aspects of human praxis as a whole. Praxis can flesh itself out in history only insofar as it takes both aspects into consideration. Bloch is looking for a religious Marxism, or a Christianity fully cognizant of its earthly dimension. In the end Bloch wants nothing less than that Marxism accept religion as its heritage: "We should raise museums to the religions of the past when they begin to serve heaven on earth and to keep the will to heaven alive not in an atmosphere of opium smoke but in the atmosphere of a religion devoid of lies."[21]

Bloch maintains that religion will exercise its true function for the first time when it does so within a socialist society. Only then will it be able to raise and respond to the acute problems centered around our yearnings for the hereafter.

Even when no clerical class exists any longer, the questions of *Whence* and *Whither* will continue to arise anxiously in a classless society. If those prove to be the great questions, and if they are as inescapable as they are today, then perhaps the church, not the church of today, . . . but an educational force teaching people about the *Whither* . . . will shed some light on this question and not allow us to rest in peace even after our work is done. . . . The more meaningful everyday life is, the more questionable death will be as an opaque intrusion into its center . . . and the more worthy of negotiation will be the space in which human life rises upward. . . .[22]

Bloch strongly objects to the dogmatic character of Marxist atheism. He calls atheism "an administrative ideal" which Marxism took over from the bourgeoisie.[23] Bloch thinks that a society of absolute atheists is impossible, that Marx's own atheism was merely a working hypothesis that will disappear with the advent of socialism.[24] He wants Marxism to ally itself with religion and not to forget the hereafter in its study of the here and now. Christians and socialists should unite, for they will find their own identity only when they do:

Socialism and Christianity have many kinds of concordance, especially in the most important matters. It is good that it is so, both in order to give depth to the avowal of socialism as well as—and perhaps even more important—to give the avowal of Christianity a sign of genuineness, and in such a manner that a new era of Christianity will be indicated, one which will light the way as the light of hope: a new era in which the kingdom of the Son of Man will occur not merely as something "above." If the salvation in the Gospel is to become flesh—for us or for men who follow—there must not be merely something above, but also something before us.[25]

The ideas of the French Marxist *Roger Garaudy* are probably better known than those of Bloch. He was one of the pioneers in Marxist-Christian dialogue, and he was a sharp critic of Russia's dogmatic Marxism. His own ideas caused him to be expelled from the Communist Party. Garaudy sees no reason why the advent of socialism should lead to the establishment of atheism as the state religion. Both Engels and Lenin, he notes, were solidly opposed to the idea of writing atheism into the statutes of the Party. Both claimed this was an anarchic proposition.[26]

In 1966 a group of Marxists and Christians gathered in Salzburg to dailogue with each other. At that meeting Garaudy talked on one occasion about Marx's dictum that religion is the opiate of the people. While insisting that there certainly was historical validity to the assertion, he pointed out that there was no reason why the Marxist conception of religion should be limited to that dictum.[27] In another book he tells us that religion becomes an opiate when "it asserts that eternal life is the essential thing, when it devaluates this present life and the struggles of history, . . . when it views the relationship between God and man as that between master and slave, . . . and when it poses as an ideology, a conception of the world, a metaphysics."[28]

Garaudy is opposed to this way of understanding and living religion. He thinks that faith can be something else, not a way of thinking but a way of living. When faith is a way of living dedicated to the creation of a better world, then it is a leaven rather than an opiate. Then "a Christian can be a complete revolutionary, not in spite of his faith but thanks to it."[29]

One of his recent works, *L'Alternative,* contains whole passages that amount to an astonishing profession of faith. He even suggests that this faith has always been implicit in his life, that it has guided all his efforts to create a more human world:

When a man has professed atheism for so many years, it is terribly upsetting for him to discover the Christian that he has been carrying inside himself all along. It is terribly upsetting to accept the responsibility of that hope. When one has been an active party member for thirty-six years, and one of its leaders for twenty years, when one has found meaning and beauty for one's life for so long within its ranks, it is a cause of anxiety to discover that one must question the whole conception of the party in order to realize the hopes which it engendered in the first place.[30]

In an earlier passage of the same work Garaudy wrote:

The real alternative to a religion that serves as the opiate of the people is not a positivist atheism, for positivism means a world not only without God but also without man. The real alternative is a militant and creative faith for which the real is not just what exists already but all the possibilities of a future that seems impossible to those who do not possess the power of hope. . . . For a whole lifetime I have been asking myself if I am a Christian, and for forty years I have answered no. The reason is that the problem was badly posed, as if faith were incompatible with the life of an activist. I am sure now and henceforth that the two are one and the same, and that my hope as a militant would have had no foundation without that faith.[31]

I certainly am in favor of a sincere dialogue with such new kinds of Marxist and atheistic humanists. I am even more in favor of joint praxis with them. For they truly love humanity as they seek for a more human way of life and "a future without God." They generously accept the idea of risking their lives and committing themselves without hope of reward. They should help to inspire Christians to commit themselves sincerely to their neighbors, to give up looking for a "God without human beings" or a "God without a future." For commitment to neighbor is the only way to find God, just as the building of a more human earth is the only way to fashion heaven.

Notes

1. Much of this chapter, too, appeared in my previous book entitled *La Revolución con Marx y con Cristo* (Caracas: Monte Avila, 1973).

2. Ignace Lepp, *Atheism in Our Time* (New York: Macmillan, 1964), p. 68.

3. Lucretius, *De Rerum Natura.*

4. Cited by Henri de Lubac, *The Drama of Atheist Humanism,* Eng. trans. (Cleveland: Meridian Books, 1967), p. 17.

5. Cited by Jean Yves Calvez, *La Pensée de Karl Marx* (Paris: Seuil, 1956), pp. 56–58.

6. Karl Marx, Dissertation on the difference between the natural philosophies of Democritus and Epicurus.

7. Marx and Engels, *The German Ideology.* There are various English translations of Marx's works. A new complete edition of his writings in English is now being published in hardcover and softcover by International Publishers and Random House.

8. See Marx, *Early Writings* (New York: McGraw-Hill, 1963), p. 45. Feuerbach's formula, which appears in his *Provisional Theses,* is "Thought is born of being, not being of thought."

9. See Marx, *Early Writings,* p. 43.

10. F. Engels, *Anti-Dühring* (Moscow: Foreign Languages Publishing House, 1959), p. 461.

11. Marx, *Early Writings,* see p. 122.

12. See ibid., p. 125.

13. Ibid., p. 44.

14. Ibid.

15. F. Engels, *Anti-Dühring*, p. 355.

16. See Marx and Engels, *Basic Writings on Politics and Philosophy*, edited by Lewis Feuer (New York: Peter Smith, 1959), pp. 268–69.

17. See Diego Oviedo, "Marx: Alienación religiosa, alienación humana," *Proyección, Teología y Mundo Actual* 17 (December 1970): 259–60.

18. See Lucio Lombardo Radice, *Socialismo y libertad* (Bilbao: Desclée de Brouwer, 1971), p. 166; original Italian edition: *Socialismo e libertà* (Rome: Riuniti, 1968).

19. See J. B. Metz, "The Future of Man: An Answer to Roger Garaudy," *Journal of Ecumenical Studies* 4 (1967): 233.

20. Ernst Bloch, *Geist der Utopie* (Berlin, 1923), p. 325.

21. Ernst Bloch, *Erbschaft dieser Zeit* (Zurich: Oprecht and Helbling, 1938), p. 10f. Cited also in Manfred Buhr, "A Critique of Ernst Bloch's Philosophy of Hope," *Philosophy Today* 14 (Winter 1970): 263.

22. See Buhr, ibid., p. 264.

23. Ernst Bloch, *Geist der Utopie*, p. 326.

24. Ibid., p. 362.

25. Ernst Bloch, "Man as Possibility," in *Cross Currents* 18 (1968): 283.

26. See R. Garaudy, "Creative Freedom," in *The Christian-Marxist Dialogue*, ed. Paul Oestreicher (New York: Macmillan Paperbacks, 1969).

27. R. Garaudy, "Christian-Marxist Dialogue," *Journal of Ecumenical Studies* (1967): 210. For the Salzburg dialogues see *Marxistes et Chrétiens. Entretiens de Salzbourg* (Paris: Mame, 1968).

28. See R. Garaudy, *La reconquista de la esperanza*, Spanish edition (Caracas: Monte Avila, 1972), pp. 98–101; French edition: *Reconquête de l'espoir* (Paris: Grasset, 1971).

29. Ibid., pp. 103 and 105.

30. R. Garaudy, *L'Alternative* (Paris: Robert Laffont, 1972), pp. 245–46; Eng. trans.: *The Alternative Future* (New York: Simon and Schuster, 1974).

31. Ibid., pp. 122 and 126.

10

GOD VERSUS HUMAN FREEDOM: SARTRE

*I am a human being, Jupiter. . . . Once freedom has ex-
ploded in the heart of a human being, the gods cannot do
anything against him.*

—Orestes in *The Flies*

Sartre seeks to champion human freedom, an absolute and
total freedom that necessarily entails the rejection of God.
Paissac sums up Sartre's philosophy of God in these terms:
"God does not exist because man is free. If God existed, he
would annul man's freedom. But since it cannot be denied that
man is free, God does not exist."[1]
Sartre is not the first to see incompatibility between human
freedom and the existence of God. Arthur Schopenhauer, for
example, maintained that divine omnipotence could not coexist with human freedom:

One might be able to talk about being created on the one hand and
being free in will and activity on the other, but it is really unimagina-
ble. For the one who called a being into existence would have to fix its
essence as well, to establish all the features of its complete being. . . . A
free being must be an original being, not a created one. If our will is
free, then it is also original entity (*das Urwesen*), and vice-versa.[2]

Bakunin offers us one of the most clear-cut examples of postulatory atheism. He reasons thus: Either God exists and we are slaves whose freedom has been expropriated by God, or else God does not exist and we are free; for the sake of revolution, however, we wish and need to be free, hence God cannot exist.

According to Sartre, God cannot exist because the freedom that tradition attributed to God actually belongs to human beings.[3] Sartre's conception of human freedom leaves no room for God. Freedom is creative, radical, constitutive. It is absolute because no one and nothing else can snatch it away from us. Even under torture we can still say No. In its very essence freedom is negative because it is the capacity to say No, but it is a creative negativity. Since human existence makes sense only as the capacity to say No, in saying No we create our world and realize ourselves in freedom.

Furthermore, human freedom is possible only because we are mortal. If we were immortal, then we could never escape the presence and power of God. The dictum, "if we are free, God does not exist," can thus be translated: "If we are free, we are mortal." The point is that we can choose our own death.

In *The Republic of Silence* Sartre recounts his recollection of the years 1940 to 1945, when he was an active member of the French Resistance. There he clarifies many of his ideas about freedom. At one point he says:

We were never more free than during the German occupation. . . . Because the Nazi venom seeped into our thoughts, every accurate thought was a conquest. Because an all-powerful police tried to force us to hold our tongues, every word took on the value of a declaration of principles. Because we were hunted down, every one of our gestures had the weight of a solemn commitment. . . . At every instant we lived up to the full sense of this commonplace little phrase: "Man is mortal!" And the choice that each of us made of his life was an authentic choice because it was made face to face with death, because it could always have been expressed in these terms: "Rather death than. . . . "[4]

In short, Sartre wants to restore to humanity the kind of freedom that Descartes had thought belonged only to God.

Descartes would have done the same, says Sartre, if he had not been confined by the theological and religious prejudices and convictions of his time.

The Cartesian God is the freest God one can imagine. He is not subordinated to the essences of beings. Instead he creates them and forces them to be what they are. This God even transcends the laws of logic and mathematics, for he can make a truth of mathematics false. To put it a different way, the truths of mathematics are truths only because God wills it. Nothing can be true prior to God's knowledge, for willing and knowing are one and the same act in God. In willing a thing God knows it, and the thing is true because God wills it.

However, this freedom really is proper to human beings, says Sartre. Human freedom is absolute, creative autonomy. It took centuries for humanity to dare to take possession of the creative liberty that Descartes had attributed to God. But finally we came to appreciate the fundamental truth of humanism:

Man is the being who causes the existence of the world. We should not censure Descartes for attributing to God what really belongs to man, however. Instead we should admire him for stressing the demands and implications of the idea of autonomy and for realizing, long before Heidegger, . . . that freedom is the one and only foundation of being.[5]

To follow Sartre's line of thought more closely, we must plunge into his ontology and consider at least some of the main ideas of *Being and Nothingness*. As we know, Sartre distinguishes between two types of beings, the being-in-itself (*être en soi*) and the being-for-itself (*être pour soi*). The things of this world are beings *en soi:* massive, opaque, closed, full of themselves, pure passivity, identical with themselves, with no reason for being, without relations to other beings because they lack consciousness and are eternally superfluous.[6]

To be a subject is equivalent to being free. The free being is a being *pour soi.* Unlike the being *en soi,* it is conscious, it transcends its own being, it is related to other beings, and it is ever caught in the tension of yesterday or tomorrow. It is *nothing* because the term "being" is reserved in Sartre's ontology for the being *en soi*. The being *pour soi* is completely different. Above all, it is *not* the deterministic result of material processes and forces. It is free to realize itself as it wishes, free to utter its "No." Hence Sartre can say that at its roots "freedom coincides with the nothingness which lies buried in the heart of man."[7] Our nonbeing isolates and differentiates us from the causal order of the world.

If being a subject means being free, then human existence, the realization of our own project, must take place in freedom. Being free, then, is not so much obtaining what one wills as determining one's own will; it is the autonomy of choosing. Freedom is not being able or unable to carry out certain actions; it is a matter of willing them or not willing them. Understood thus, it is obvious that we are absolute freedom; for no one and no thing can force us to will or choose something else. Hence we also bear absolute responsibility. We are responsible for ourselves and the world because we and only we, through the acts of our freedom, are the authors of ourselves and the world.

Thus we are also responsible for everything that happens to us. If I go to war, it is because I choose to go to war. I am responsible for the war because I could desert or kill myself. It is as if "I myself had declared the war."[8] Refusing to perform certain actions is choosing, is being free. In the last analysis we cannot not choose, for even our non-choosing is choosing not to choose. Condemned to absolute freedom and hence absolutely responsible, we are beings who live in a state of permanent anxiety.

Since we are absolutely free and absolutely responsible, we are also the norm and fountainhead of morality as well as the only creator of values. There are no norms or values written in heaven because there is no God to write them there.[9] My freedom is the sole foundation of values. Nothing, absolutely nothing, justifies my adoption of one particular set of values.[10] The dictum in *The Brothers Karamazov*, "If there is no God, then everything is permitted," is the starting point for the existentialist. It is we who create our own values and our own morality.

In the last analysis it does not matter whether one chooses to forge a new civilization as Alexander the Great did, or whether one chooses to be a drunken bum. Even the latter choice can be a loftier attitude if it is realized with a greater degree of freedom. Since we are free, we have only one norm and one law: our own freedom. When Electra's sister submits to Jupiter in *The Flies* and becomes his slave, she becomes the perfect embodiment of antihumanism. Orestes typifies the human being who is fully conscious of his freedom and enamored of it. In his human pride he boldly stands up to Jupiter: "I am a human being, Jupiter. . . . Once freedom has exploded in the heart of a human being, the gods cannot do anything against him."[11]

Sartre vigorously rejects Christian morality and its norms "inscribed in man's conscience." As expressions of the will of God, they end up castrating activity based on freedom. He vividly presents his criticism of Christian morality in his play entitled *Le Diable et le Bon Dieu,* which is set in the context of Germany during the Reformation. Goetz is besieging the city of Worms, and he is ready to slay its 20,000 inhabitants in order to see if God will come to the defense of his own poor and oppressed. Under the urgings of the priest Heinrich, however, he raises his siege and decides to change his mind. Heinrich tells him that man can only do evil, that all good has already been done by God the Father. Goetz asserts that he will be the first human being to do good. He retires to the woods and inflicts severe mortifications on his own body. Then Heinrich arrives to tell him that the barons have defeated the peasants and that 25,000 have been slain. His main purpose in coming, however, is to tell Goetz that it was just as wicked of him to lacerate his soul with ascetic tortures as to be complacent with it. No matter what he does, man does evil. God is not the least bit interested in what human beings do, whether he kisses the lips of a prostitute or a leper, dies of penances or of lustful excesses.[12]

Goetz suddenly realizes that he has been living in a web of illusions. He looked to heaven for some sign but found no response whatsoever. God is the silence that we confront, our loneliness. It is we who choose evil and invent good, and only we can pardon ourselves. If God exists, then we are nothing. But the fact is that God does not exist.[13] It is all a colossal joke. There is no longer any heaven or hell. God is dead and we are left all alone.[14] We alone are responsible for our actions. Morality and justice are human affairs.

There are other reasons why Sartre feels that God must be rejected. If God existed, he would be our creator. That would mark the end of human freedom for then we would have an essence and our whole life would be fixed ahead of time in accordance with some divine pattern. We would be a work of art already finished and signed.[15] Such a possibility is out of the question, says Sartre. Existence takes priority over essence, and we are what we make of ourselves.[16] We are free to create ourselves and to make what we will out of our creation, hence God cannot possibly exist.

Another reason why Sartre rejects God has to do with his view of "the Other." If God existed, he would be the Other par excellence. What is "the Other"? It is someone who looks at me and thereby annihilates my subjectivity.[17] I am thereby reduced to a thing, so that my transcendence and my freedom are stifled. I am reduced to a being *en soi,* because to the Other I appear stripped of my transcendence.[18] How can I evade this objectifying, reifying look? Only by looking at the Other in turn, thereby converting the Other into my object. Thus conflict is the essential note of human relationships, not "being with" as Heidegger affirms.[19]

This point is made vividly in his play entitled *No Exit.* The action takes place in the metaphorical hell of a drawing room furnished in the style of the Second Empire. Doomed to live together are a servant, a journalist, and two young women. One of the women is a homosexual, the other is heterosexual. Under each other's reifying glances, their liberty is annihilated. They are caught in an eternal war of possessing a being possessed. No one of them can escape the objectifying looks of the others: "Hell is other people."

Now if God existed, he would be the Other par excellence. His omnipresent glance would completely destroy our freedom. We would have to live eternally as alienated and reified beings. To be free, active subjects, we must reject God. In his autobiography Sartre describes how he experienced God in these terms as a child and quickly rejected him:

Once only I had the feeling that He existed. I had been playing with matches and had burnt a mat. I was busy covering up my crime when suddenly God saw me. I felt His gaze inside my head and on my hands. I turned round and round in the bathroom, horribly visible, a living target. I was saved by indignation. I grew angry at such a crude lack of tact, and blasphemed. . . . He never looked at me again.[20]

One cannot help but wonder over Sartre's idea of God. His God is a being with an infinite, reifying gaze who prevents us from exercising freedom and attaining fulfillment as a subject. His image of God reminds us of his image of his own hieratic grandfather: Sartre tells us that his grandfather looked like pictures of God the Father and was often taken for him. But he had mellowed by the time that Sartre appeared on the scene. If he had begotten Jean Paul, he would have enslaved him. But the presence of Jean Paul as his grandchild pleased him, and the old man adored him: "Did he love me? I find it hard to tell sincerity from artifice in so public an emotion. I do not think he showed much affection for his other grandsons. It is true that he hardly ever saw them and that they had no need of him. But I depended on him for everything. He adored, in me, his generosity."[21]

Sartre never seems to have gotten over his early image of God as an enslaving being who found narcissistic satisfaction in the dependence of others on him. But it is the image of a false God, an idol. The real God wills freedom for us and invites us to share in his own life of love. The God of biblical revelation gazes on human beings with love. Moved by our sorrows, God takes his stand with us and helps them to achieve human fulfillment. To love is to will that the other be an active subject. Being loved helps rather than hinders one's self-fulfillment in freedom. In the loving gaze of another, one can find one's own being and dignity. To love another person is to accept and acknowledge his or her distinctiveness as a person. Things are not loved. Only subjects, only persons, can be objects of love.

The loving gaze of God is an invitation to freedom, a summons to live out our own project with an absolute Thou who guarantees our own life as real subjects. He asks us to live in communion with him in and through the Thou of every human being, so that relationships between beings mean brotherhood rather than hell.

Finally, for Sartre the very idea of God entails a contradiction. It combines and brings together the idea of the being *en soi* and the idea of the being *pour soi*. Those ideas are contradictory and mutually exclusive. The being *en soi* is self-sufficient being which stands in need of nothing. Isn't that what God is, asks Sartre, a being who is pure positivity and the foundation of the world?[22] At the same time, however, God must be a conscious being, a being *pour soi*, who lacks everything and is nothing. So God must be both pure positivity and pure negativity, complete independence and complete dependence, plenitude and emptiness, relationship and nonrelationship. God is simply our own anxiety-ridden projection, our frustrated attempt to combine the *pour soi* and the *en soi* within ourselves.

We struggle to be God. All our effort is enlisted to acquire an essence, to identify the void of our consciousness with the plenitude of things. Since it is impossible for us to synthesize these two contradictory terms, we are an "abortive God," a "useless passion."

Little remains to be said here except that we do not envision the idol of Sartre's philosophy when we talk about faith in God here. It is obvious enough that one can prove that the idea of God entails a contradiction if one starts off from Sartre's ontological premises. But quite aside from the fact that it is doubtful that any philosophy can either prove or disprove the existence of God, there is some question about the validity of Sartre's own principles and conclusions. As William Luijpen suggests, it may well be that his own principles are contradictory.[23] What about the "plenitude of being" that Sartre accords the being *en soi*? If we view the latter in phenomenological terms, we certainly cannot see any fullness of being in it. Certainly not in the sense of "aseity" that we attribute to God. The plenitude of being we find in a rock is hardly the plenitude we affirm in our concept of God. Nor do we conceive a being *pour soi* as pure nothingness. In the last analysis the being that Sartre finds to be contradictory in terms of his own ontology is something very different from the being that the believer calls God.[24]

In conclusion we might also ask whether there is not a great deal of superficiality to be found in Sartre's idol-god who gazes oppressively on humanity. Is it possible that his whole atheism rests upon a very superficial foundation? Another passage in his autobiography suggests such a possibility:

One morning, in 1917, at La Rochelle, I was waiting for some companions who were supposed to accompany me to the *lycée*. They were late. Soon I could think of nothing more to distract myself, and I decided to think about the Almighty. He at once tumbled down into the blue sky and vanished without explanation. He does not exist, I said to myself, in polite astonishment, and I thought the matter was settled. In one sense it was, because I have never since had the least temptation to revive Him.[25]

Sartre's godless philosophy ends up with a concept of the human being as unjustified and unjustifiable, an absurdity, a useless passion. We are frustrated in our dream to be God, caught in an antagonistic relationship with our fellows, and immersed in a world that causes nausea. Sartre liberates us by plunging us into his own meaninglessness. Over against such ideas stands the word of God summoning us to live out our freedom and to create the fullness of the kingdom in joint fellowship with others.

Notes

1. H. Paissac, *Le dieu de Sartre* (Grenoble: Arthaud, 1950), p. 16f.

2. A. Schopenhauer, *Werke*, VIII, p. 215f.

3. Jean Paul Sartre, *Situations* (Paris: Gallimard, 1947), 1:314f.; Eng. trans.: *Situations* (New York: Braziller, 1965).

4. Cited by William Barrett in *Irrational Man: A Study in Existential Philosophy* (New York: Doubleday Anchor Books, 1958), pp. 213–14.

5. Sartre, *René Descartes, Discours de la Méthode* (Paris, 1948), p. 203f.

6. Sartre, *L'être et le néant* (Paris: Gallimard, 1949). See Eng. trans., *Being and Nothingness*, pp. lxv-lxvi.

7. Ibid., p. 440.

8. Ibid., p. 555.

9. See Sartre, *Existentialism and Humanism*, Eng. trans. (London: Methuen, 1948), p. 33.

10. Sartre, *L'être et le néant;* see Eng. trans. p. 38.

11. Sartre, *Les Mouches* (Paris: Theatre, 1947), pp. 11-13; Eng. trans.: *No Exit and Three Other Plays* (New York: Vintage, 1956).

12. Sartre, *Le Diable et le Bon Dieu;* Eng. trans., *The Devil and the Good Lord* (New York: Knopf, 1960), p. 141.

13. Ibid., see page 143 of the Eng. trans.

14. Ibid.

15. See Sartre, *Les Mots* (Paris, 1963), p. 78.

16. Sartre, *Existentialism and Humanism*, p. 28.

17. Sartre, *L'être et le néant;* see Eng. trans., p. 257.

18. See ibid., p. 262.

19. Sartre's sociology, as it is elaborated in his *Critique de la raison dialectique,* generally follows this same line of thought. Human beings are marked by "necessity." To combat necessity, they must come together in work societies where they compete with each other. Faced with the scarcity that typifies our world, they find that what one possesses is something of which others are deprived or robbed. Thus people become capable of robbing and killing each other. Each individual sees his fellow as an Other, as a principle of evil. Society enshrines the impossibility of coexistence, denies one's own being, and thus is the very embodiment of evil.

20. Sartre, *Les Mots;* Eng. trans.: *Words* (London: Penguin Books, 1967), p. 65.

21. Ibid., p. 17.

22. Sartre, *L'être et le néant;* see Eng. trans., p. 90.

23. William A. Luijpen, *Phenomenology and Atheism* (Pittsburgh: Dusquesne University Press, 1964), p. 289.

24. Perhaps no one has answered Sartre better on this point than his compatriot Merleau-Ponty. He points out that there is no sense to a being *pour soi* apart from an object, and no sense to a being *en soi* apart from a subject. See *Phenomenology of Perception,* Eng. trans. (London: Routledge, 1962), pp. 61-63; also *Sens et non-sens* (Paris: Nagel, 1948), p. 187; Eng. trans.: *Sense and Non-sense* (Evanston: Northwestern University Press, 1964).

25. Sartre, *Les Mots;* Eng. trans., p. 155.

11

GOD AS SURETY
FOR SUFFERING
AND ABSURDITY: CAMUS

If a massive death defines the human condition . . . then
the metaphysical rebel is more a blasphemer than an
atheist. In the name of order he blasphemes, denouncing
God as the father of death and the supreme outrage.
— Albert Camus

Camus was undoubtedly a fascinating personality. It is easy
to see why thousands of young people looked upon him as
their hero and why all of France felt a deep loss when he was
killed in a car crash. Camus was an intense, honest person who
preached about the existential absurdity of the human condition. As Sir Herbert Read put it, he was the leader of "man's
metaphysical rebellion against the conditions of life and
against life itself." Looking squarely in the face of doubt,
despair, and nihilism, he refused to succumb to them.[1] A man
of generous soul, he took sides with those who were suffering
and oppressed. He rebelled against the suffering of children
and innocents and united himself with the atheism of the
laboring class. As he said in *The Rebel,* the working masses
oppressed by suffering and death are masses without God, and
our proper place is at their side.

The absurdity of life is the starting point of Camus's philosophy. Just as Sartre's character Antoine Roquentin is overwhelmed by the meaningless of existence, so Camus feels overwhelmed by the absurdity of life and the pointless monotony of everyday activity. You get up every morning, take the bus, go to work, go to lunch, then back to work, and so forth. Then suddenly one day you ask yourself "Why?" and are filled with boredom and disgust.[2]

The sense of absurdity does not just come from the fact that the world does not seem to have any meaning. It also stems from our capacity to see the lack of harmony, the suffering of the innocent, and the injustice in the world, while knowing full well that we cannot really do anything about them. As Camus puts it:

Man can dominate almost everything that should be dominated. He ought to rectify everything in creation that is to be rectified. But even after doing all that, children will go on dying in the most perfect society. Even with the greatest of effort man can only hope to diminish the suffering in the world arithmetically. Injustice and suffering will remain. No matter how confined they are, they will never cease to be an outrage. Dimitri Karamozov's cry, "Why?" will continue to echo throughout history. Art and rebellion will die out only with the death of the last man on earth.[3]

Man, says Camus, would erase suffering from the world if he could. Hence we cannot tolerate the idea of a God who does not exterminate the evil in the world even though he can.

Camus's literary works, particularly *The Fall* and *The Stranger,* capture the sense of absurdity in marvellously vivid terms. *The Fall* captures the absurdity and emptiness of bourgeois life. The main character, Clemence, possesses all the things that most people dream of possessing: wealth, a good position, luck, and success with women. He is a bourgeois Parisian, an egotistical man who is all surface and empty inside. One day he adverts to his own emptiness and is filled with nausea. Finding himself incapable of plunging in to rescue a drowning girl, he becomes convinced that in reality he has never been able to love other human beings. On the bridges of Paris, he confesses,

I also learned that I was afraid of my freedom. . . . Freedom is not a reward, a triumph to be celebrated with champagne. . . . It is a task, an exhausting long-distance race that one must run alone. No cham-pagne, no friends raising their glasses and giving you an affectionate glance. One must decide alone, in the face of oneself or of the judgment of another. And at the end of all freedom stands a condemnatory tribunal. That is why freedom is so heavy to bear, especially if one is oppressed, feverish, or does not love anyone.[4]

Having nothing to live for and no God to turn to, Clemence tries to find some liberating penance by proclaiming his own guilt to the patrons of the Mexico City Bar in Amsterdam. The abasement of his life there is more authentic than the empty facade of his earlier bourgeois life.

Mersault, the main character of *The Stranger,* embodies the absurdity of life as such. His life is simple and unpretentious. He perfectly typifies the modern man who, as Clemence might say, "fornicates and reads the newspaper." He has a fiancée, a little place of his own, the beach, and his work. His friends are so-so friends. The death of his mother is an embarrassment for him rather than an occasion of sorrow, for it forces him to change his living routine somewhat. He does not feel any emotion about it, and he does not try to manufacture any. He goes to the burial service because he "has to." He feels drowsy and almost falls asleep in front of her corpse.

One hot day Mersault kills an Arab. But the deed seems more like something that happened to him than something he himself did. The crime was born of instinct rather than of will. It takes a terrible effort to keep recalling what happened and telling it to one person after another. They may do what they want with him, but he wants to be left alone and unmolested. He is found guilty and condemned to death, not so much for his crime as for the fact that he did not weep at his mother's funeral. As Leslie Paul puts it: "His destruction by guillotine becomes necessary to society in the story, not because he is guilty, but because society is affronted by his nakedness."[5] And summing up his view of the work, Paul says: "Perhaps . . . Camus succeeds in showing forth *l'acte gratuit* and the struggle for sincerity which haunt all André Gide's writings: he was the first to explore moral sclerosis. But the net impact, despite that failure of nerve which made Camus soften Mersault's execution with a breath of cosmic happiness, is of the senselessness of living."[6]

The Misunderstanding is a play which also deals with the absurdity of life and the impact of human egotism. After many years away from home, Jan returns home to his mother and sister. Since they do not recognize him, he waits for an opportune moment to reveal his identity to them. He tells his wife: "You can't remain a stranger all your life. It is certainly true that human beings need happiness, but they also need to find their true place in the world."[7]

His sister and mother think he is a very wealthy man. They kill him to get his money. When they discover who their victim is, they commit suicide. Toward the end his sister and murderer exclaims: "All I want is to be left in peace with my rage, my rightful rage. I have no intention of . . . asking for forgiveness before I die. I hate this cramped world in which I have been denied my rights. . . . I will not bend my knees."[8]

Maria, Jan's wife, kneels and prays when the impact of the tragedy hits her. An old servant hears her praying and comes to ask if she had called him. She turns to him for help as she had just turned to God. The servant simply answers "No" and goes off, leaving her alone. She is left alone with her sorrow and her desperation in a strange town, among people who do not even know her. As the drama ends, she is raising her arms in vain toward an empty heaven and a God that does not exist.[9]

But Camus's philosophy does not stop with the absurdity of life. It also seeks to transcend that absurdity. Once human beings realize that absurdity surrounds them, they must immediately decide whether life has meaning or not. That is why Camus asserts, in *The Myth of Sisyphus,* that suicide is the one and only serious philosophic problem. Deciding whether life is meaningful or not is the essential question of every philosophy.

If we choose suicide, however, we absolutize absurdity and allow it to triumph over us. Instead Camus chooses rebellion, an attitude of firm challenge and tension and a constant struggle against suicide. To rebel is to believe in life in spite of everything. It is to assert that struggle and effort itself is meaningful. The rebel fashions solidarity among all rebels, engaging in life's own struggle against life. The "No" of the rebel is not a renunciation, for the rebel feels in some way that he is right and that something is worth toil and effort. In the last analysis the rebel chooses to accept the final failure of death rather than be despoiled of his freedom. It is better to die on one's feet than to live on one's knees. In his act of rebellion a man identifies himself with all other rebels and thereby transcends his own loneliness and solitude. The first step forward for a human being, who is faced with the absurdity of things, is to realize that his own feelings are shared by other human beings: "I rebel, therefore we exist."[10]

Camus distinguishes two kinds of rebellion: historical rebellion and metaphysical rebellion. Historical rebellion is a protest against specific living conditions and circumstances. Metaphysical rebellion is much more radical and important. It is a protest against the human condition itself. In it man cries out against his own condition and all creation, against the suffering of life and death, against the lack of fulfillment due to death and the meaninglessness due to evil: "If a massive death defines the human condition . . . then the metaphysical rebel is more a blasphemer than an atheist. In the name of order he blasphemes, denouncing God as the father of death and the supreme outrage."[11]

Camus brings new ardor and force to the old argument against God's existence that is based on the evil existing in the world. He prefers to deny the existence of a God who would have to bear the responsibility for not eradicating evil if he did exist. His concept of God is that of a monster who pays no heed to the suffering of his creatures. Human rebels, by contrast, display heroism and brotherly humanism even as they react against God. They turn their face toward human beings to share their struggles and their misery. The cry of Camus is that of Dimitri Karamazov: "If all are not going to be saved, what does my own salvation matter." The rebel rejects God and divinity in order to share in the struggles of all human beings.

The earth is to be our first and last love; on it all people live and breathe together. Secure in this knowledge, we can remake the soul of our time. We shall try to fashion the unity of the world even without God.[12]

For Camus rebellion becomes a kind of new religion. It is a passionate search for a new God, for something that will give meaning to life and explain the absurdity of worldly suffering. Faced with a world condemned to death and the impenetrable opaqueness of the human condition, the rebel calls for a new life and absolute clear-sightedness.[13]

There is no hope of success or victory, of course, but rebellion is the only motive for humanism, joy, and life. In his will to engage in the struggle of being human, Camus reminds us of Nietzsche. Humanity is like the mythical Sisyphus, who must eternally roll a boulder to the top of a mountain and watch it tumble back down time and again. But the struggle to reach the top is enough to satisfy the human heart, and so we must imagine Sisyphus to be happy.[14]

Camus's best novel, *The Plague*, is a fine epitome of his whole philosophy. The absurd appears in the form of a plague of rats in the town of Oran (Algeria). The death toll mounts to about thirty people a day, most of them children. But a group of rebels choose to fight the plague to the end: Rieux, an atheist doctor; Paneloux, a Jesuit priest tormented by the suffering of the innocent; Rambert, a journalist who chooses to stay and fight the disease; and Tarrou, somewhat akin to Dostoyevsky's Kirillov, a humanist who wants to be a saint without God and who dies from the plague. Because they join together in rebellion, these people live out an authentic, fraternal humanism. Their fight gives meaning to their lives despite the chilling anxiety that fills their hearts. They know that the plague can never be conquered completely because it is imbedded in human hearts, but still they do not stop fighting against it. Their fight is a triumph against absurdity and evil, even though there is no chance of ultimate victory.

When Tarrou asks the doctor if he believes in God, the doctor says that he does not but that it doesn't really matter. It is death that stares us in the face, and it would be better for human beings to forget about God and pit all their efforts against death. There will be no lasting victory, but that is no reason to stop fighting. Tarrou asks the doctor who taught him all that. The doctor answers simply: suffering.[15]

Rebellion, however, must also have its proper limits. Camus tells us that it should take into account the welfare of other human beings and be acted out in solidarity with them. This is brought out in one of his plays entitled *Caligula.* The Roman emperor rebels against his own emptiness and his life situation in attempting to attain happiness; but he does so in an excessively individualistic and twisted way. He executes his subjects indiscriminately, starves out whole villages, and demands to be revered as a God. He soon comes to realize, however, that this is not the way to realize his freedom or to find happiness. He is alone with his cold glory, and he realizes that he has gone down the wrong road. His kind of freedom is not good.

Behind the despotic figure of Caligula we can readily detect Hitler or any other tyrant who dreams of being a superman. Unlike Nietzsche, who might have been inclined to exalt such a figure, Camus is a man in rebellion against every oppression. With no hope in God, he embraces the suffering and wounded heart of humanity and makes its suffering his own.

Simone Weil once wrote: "Of two human beings who have not experienced God in their lives, the one who denies him may be closer to him than the one who affirms him."[16] Even with his denial of God, the generous-hearted Camus may have been very close to God. He rebelled not so much against God as against evil and suffering, and he invited all human beings to fight against them in united solidarity. His thinking is eminently Christian. He did not realize that God, too, is in favor of the oppressed and against all types of oppression. But God summons human beings to join together with him in combatting it rather than eliminating it gratuitously. Christianity stands in the same vein of generosity and combat as Camus did. The main difference lies in Camus's pessimism. Faced with that, Christianity counters with the sureness of a definitive victory against absurdity and evil, a victory won in the cross of Christ.

Notes

1. Eugene Fontinelli, "Reflections on Faith and Metaphysics," in *Speaking of God,* ed. D. Dirscherl (Milwaukee: Bruce, 1967), p. 119.

2. See Albert Camus, *The Myth of Sisyphus,* Eng. trans. (New York: Vintage Books, 1956), pp. 106ff.

3. See Camus, *L'homme révolté;* Eng. trans., *The Rebel* (New York: Knopf, 1954).

4. See Albert Camus, *The Fall,* Eng. trans. (New York: Vintage Books, 1956), pp. 132–33.

5. Leslie Paul, *Alternatives to Christian Belief* (New York: Doubleday & Company, 1967), p. 174.

6. Ibid., p. 175.

7. A. Camus, *Le malentendu;* for an Eng. trans. see *The Misunderstanding* (New York: Vintage Books, 1958), p. 87.

8. Ibid., see page 125 in the Eng. trans.

9. See Anthony Padovano, *The Estranged God: Modern Man's Search for Belief* (New York: Sheed and Ward, 1966), p. 114.

10. Camus, *L'homme révolté;* see pp. 423–32 of the Eng. trans. cited in note 3.

11. Ibid., pp. 435–36 in the Eng. trans.

12. Ibid., pp. 101 and 306 in the Eng. trans.

13. Ibid, p. 101.

14. Camus, *The Myth of Sisyphus,* see p. 123 in the Eng. edition.

15. Camus, *The Plague,* Eng. trans. (New York: Modern Library, 1948), pp. 116–18.

16. Simone Weil, *Le pesanteur et la grâce* (Paris: Plon, 1948), p. 132; Eng. trans.: *Gravity and Grace* (New York: Putnam, 1952).

12

CHRISTIANITY
AS AMBIGUITY:
MERLEAU-PONTY

It is impossible to rely on the attitude of a Christian. One can never be sure how he will act. One cannot count on him. It is impossible for the Christian to evince that basic primary sincerity because he cannot uproot equivocalness from his essence ever.

—Merleau-Ponty

Merleau-Ponty always expressed displeasure, and rightly so, when people labelled his philosophy as "atheistic." He himself felt that such a label turned it into a purely negative thing. As he himself said: "I do not waste my time and energy calling myself an atheist because I am not concerned to deny the existence of God. That would amount to turning the whole positive thrust of philosophizing into nothing but a negation."[1]

For Merleau-Ponty philosophy is a quest for meaning in the form of truth and value. This is possible because the appearance of humanity opens up the possibility of a dialogue between human beings and the world. Being has meaning insofar as it is discovered and explained by a subject; or, as Heidegger might put it, being "is" insofar as it is being "for a subject." Sartre's being *en soi,* a being without any relation to a subject, is really inconceivable.

Human beings, then, are subjects who lay hold of reality. It is through us that the world has meaning and an explanation. We ourselves, however, could never be explained in any way because we are prior to any explanation and are presupposed in it. Herein lies the marvelous enchantment of philosophy and of humanity, according to Merleau-Ponty. While everything else is explained by the subject, we ourselves must necessarily remain unexplained. Neither we nor anything human can have any explanation whatsoever. If some people find this too disconcerting and unjustifiably try to look elsewhere for a soothing explanation of humanity, Merleau-Ponty would reproach them for trying to convert philosophy into a "hospital."

Merleau-Ponty points out that the human being as a subject is not the necessary, mechanistic result of forces and processes. "It is not a cosmological factor but a place where all the cosmological factors find their meaningfulness and are historicized."[2] We are free and contingent beings; we are contingent freedom and the fountainhead of all meaningfulness. To act out human contingency and freedom is to realize history. And since we are not blind forces but "weak spots" in the heart of being, of nature, Merleau-Ponty reminds us that humankind might possibly meet with definitive failure in its historical course.

Since we are contingent freedom and cannot have any explanation, the rejection of God would seem to be implied in Merleau-Ponty's philosophy. Theology plays dirty, he tells us, because it denies human contingency at the same time it affirms it. "Theology establishes the contingency of man only in order to derive it from a necessary being. But that comes down to rejecting his contingency, for it uses the spell of philosophy to end up with an affirmation that determines him."[3] Theology affirms the existence of God as a necessary being, and it pictures this necessary being as the "cause" of human contingency. According to Merleau-Ponty, that tack implicitly reduces the human being to a necessitated being. It denies the contingency of the human subject, and hence the wondrous fact that meaning is given to the world by human subjects who themselves cannot have meaning. Thus "the contingency of man as subject cannot coexist with the idea of an infinite being who is the creator of the world." Fideistic existentialism is impossible. Marcel is illogical.

We might perhaps agree with Merleau-Ponty if philosophy were something more than a "waiting for God," as Heidegger has called it. It is a hopeful waiting that has been fulfilled by the revelation of a God who has rendered himself present in his actions. When Merleau-Ponty talks about God as "cause," he undoubtedly is thinking of the unilateral and deterministic influence that one being of nature exercises over the being of another being of nature. Viewing things in this light, his philosophy would obviously reject God as a cause. It is to be expected that a subject cannot be caused by a natural force in a natural process. As Remy C. Kwant points out, Merleau-Ponty thinks that giving an explanation of a subject would come down to linking up the contingent subject with the necessary being of God as cause of the subject. For Merleau-Ponty God would be a cause in the sense of "force," and his causality would be that of a physical process.[4]

It should be quite apparent that we cannot refer to God as cause in this mechanistic sense, although in the past some scholastic philosophers and Christians have done so. God has spoken to us of himself as love, as an absolute subject who invites us to share his life of love. Instead of annihilating a subject, love actually helps the subject to attain full self-realization. Our being is a "being with" (Heidegger), a life in community and love. It is not that of an isolated monad (Leibnitz), nor that of a being constantly attacking others or defending itself against them (Sartre).

We need to love and be loved in order to develop ourselves fully. Human beings without love are far away from their goal as human beings. In love we do not find our being determined and annihilated but rather complemented and perfected. If we are loved we are not turned into objects; instead we are treated completely as free subjects. When the causality involved is that of love, notes Luijpen, the dominant feature is the reciprocity of the subjects; and the result is not the determination of a being but rather its freedom.[5] Or, as G. Madinier has put it, "loving is willing the other as subject."[6]

It should be clear, then, that God's love does not annihilate our being as subjects. Instead he perfects it. We are subjects open to the intimacy of an ongoing, love-filled dialogue with an absolute Thou. We are loved with an infinite love that guarantees our unique value and absolute dignity despite our own infidelities and forgetfulness.

While the atheism of Merleau-Ponty's philosophy is somewhat hazy, debatable, and of little concern to him, his rejection of Christianity is open and forthright. In his opinion Christianity suffers from a basic dichotomy that will always prevent it from adopting clear, well defined attitudes. Christianity is made up of contradictions and contrarieties. It has, as it were, two Gods and two religions. There is an internal God and an external God, a religion of the Father and a religion of the Son.

In the religion of the Father, God appears as an Infinite who has full possession of us and is more intimate to us than we ourselves are. God is supreme goodness and perfection, to whom we can add nothing. God is also eternal and immutable. Viewed in this light, the temporal and the finite lose all meaningfulness. Absolute perfection is already fully realized in God, history is a closed book, time is circular, and we are already finished beings. As a result we lose our affection for this earth and this life, passively submitting ourselves to the "will of God."

With the incarnation, on the other hand, we see the start of faith in an external God and of the religion of the Son. History is sacralized because the activity of God enters it. Humanity and the world are given value once again: "God cannot be fully God and his creation cannot attain its perfection unless man recognizes God and puts all creation at his feet through faith."

It is precisely here that we find the ambiguity and dichotomy of Christianity, according to Merleau-Ponty. The lives of Christians are always fluctuating between these two opposite poles; they never are decided by either of them. Christians say that they have faith, but at the same time they wait for the findings of science to know what they are to hold on to. They are ready to die, but only to live again. Faith is a blind surrender in the darkness of night, but at the same time one knows to whom one is surrendering and one expects to see the light.

The world, history, our work, and life are both important and unimportant. They are meant to be a part of something that is already perfect. As a result Christians are in practice both conservative and revolutionary. They justify revolutions that they had previously opposed. They protest against their ministers and the church, maintaining that each individual is a minister and is the church. They can even derive good from failure by maintaining that God writes straight with crooked lines. In short "It is impossible to rely on the attitude of a Christian. One can never be sure how he will act. One cannot count on him. It is impossible for the Christian to evince that basic, primary sincerity because he cannot uproot equivocalness from his essence ever."[7] Here, then, is the paradox of Christianity, and of Catholicism in particular: "The Catholic never decides for the internal God or the external God. He always takes a stand midway between the two possibilities."[8]

This ambivalent attitude leads to many undesirable results. It fosters intolerance: "I piously kill my enemies." It rules out the possibility of dialogue: "They possess the whole truth. How can there be any genuine interchange between one who knows and one who does not?" It also leads to quietism: "If Christians possess the Truth and God, . . . then there is literally nothing to do."[9]

In short, then, Merleau-Ponty judges that Christianity must be rejected because its ambiguous and indecisive attitude entails a negation of authentic involvement and activity in the world. Christians can only be "bad conservatives" and "bad revolutionaries" because they are both at once. They are two-faced human beings who say they love this earth but who are always thinking about another world and heaven. Only by rejecting God and heaven will they be able to commit themselves truly to humanity and this earth.

Behind the thinking of Merleau-Ponty we can hear echoes of Nietzsche: "I urge you, brothers, remain faithful to this earth." But those sentiments intermingle with the sentiments of another person, a believer, who passionately loved this earth. The words of Pierre Teilhard de Chardin could be echoed by many Christians of more recent times who view their faith as a commitment rather than as an escape: "In the name of our faith we have the right and the duty to love the things of this earth passionately."

Contrary to all false and mistaken interpretations, Christians are not ones who pass by this earth without attaching any importance to it because they are obsessed with afterlife. Unfortunately Christians all too often have succumbed to distorted notions of this sort, giving way to passivism and accepting reality no matter how unjust and inhuman it might be. But authentic Christians are human beings in love with this earth. They know that they must find fulfillment for themselves in it, and that God has placed it in their hands as a task to be fulfilled. They anxiously strain to bring human beings peace, justice, and the brotherhood of the children of God. They love their fellows, not to win heaven, but because they are human beings and, what is more, their brothers and sisters.

What Merleau-Ponty calls a "dichotomy" should be called "plenitude." It is the plenitude, the full measure, of love and commitment. It is the hunger for greater justice and equality, and the effort to achieve them. If Merleau-Ponty's humanist judged it necessary to reject Christianity, it was because he himself did not understand Christianity. He succumbed to the image of Christianity conveyed by the idolatrous Christian masses. He did not manage to get beyond it to an authentic view of its human and terrestrial depths, of its profound commitment to history and the world, and of its inalienable defense of the rights and values of the human person. If there is any clear message in biblical revelation, even in the religion of the Father, it is that we are summoned to turn our lives into a vocation and a commitment to the liberation of the world and humanity. That is brought out in the very first pages of the book of Genesis.

Dostoyevsky overcame his will toward unbelief by passionately and blindly submitting to faith in Christ. In *The Brothers Karamazov* he writes:

Alyosha remained standing, possessed, then suddenly flung himself to the earth. He did not know why he was embracing it. He could not say why he was on fire to kiss it again and again. In tears he kept kissing the earth, saying that he would always love her passionately. . . . "Water the earth with the tears of your joy and love those tears," he said to himself in his soul.[10]

Christians must be like Alyosha, enamored of this earth. We must love the world and all human beings. We know that we belong to the kingdom of this world, that on it we must commit our lives to serving others. We realize that faith is not some rational body of content but a commitment of our lives, as we wait and hope for the one who overcame evil and assured us definitive victory. At the end of life all Christians should be able to adopt the words of Bernanos for their own epitaphs: "When I die, tell the kingdom of earth that I loved it more than I dared to say."[11]

Hope for fulfillment in a world hereafter can make sense only if we passionately love this world now. Christians are not meant to be conservatives who try to anchor history and hold it back. We are meant to be perduring revolutionaries, members of the kingdom that is gradually being fleshed out and fulfilled, that goes on both as presence and as promise simultaneously.

Notes

1. Merleau-Ponty, "L'homme et l'adversité," and "Deuxième entretien privé: La connaissance de l'homme au XXème siècle," in *Rencontres Internationales de Genève,* 1951, p. 250.

2. Merleau-Ponty, *Eloge de la philosophie,* p. 61; Eng. trans.: *In Praise of Philosophy* (Evanston: Northwestern University Press, 1963).

3. Ibid.

4. Remy C. Kwant, *The Phenomenological Philosophy of Merleau-Ponty,* (Pittsburgh: Duquesne University Press, 1963), p. 132f.

5. Henry J. Koren and William A. Luijpen, *A First Introduction to Existential Phenomenology* (Pittsburgh: Duquesne University Press, 1969), p. 228f.

6. G. Madinier, *Conscience et amour* (Paris, 1947), p. 25.

7. Merleau-Ponty, *Sense et non-sens* (Paris: Nagel, 1948), p. 364; Eng. trans.: *Sense and Non-sense* (Evanston: Northwestern University Press, 1964).

8. Ibid., p. 360.

9. Ibid., pp. 74 and 356.

10. F. Dostoyevsky, *The Brothers Karamazov.* There are many English editions of the novel.

11. Cited by Anthony Padovano, "American Unbelief and the Death of God," *Proceedings* of the 21st annual convention of the Catholic Theological Society of America, June 1966, Vol. 21, p. 148.

CONCLUSION

ATHEISM AS A PURIFYING
AGENT FOR CHRISTIANITY

*Atheism can be a purifying force, and faith can serve as a
substitute for courage or sincerity.*

—H. Duméry

*One can be an atheist while professing faith in God, and a
believer while professing atheism.*

—H. De Lubac

We live in a world dominated by injustice. Cruel, inhuman
injustice is pervasive. It divides humanity into the First World
and the Third World, the developed and the underdeveloped
countries, the rich and the poor, the powerful and the powerless, almsgivers and beggars. We find injustice in international
relations, within nations and peoples, in organizations, and in
every human group. It dominates people, dictates to them,
humiliates them, and turns them into a herd. We find luxury
over against wretched poverty, libertinism over against bondage, leisure over against utter exhaustion, and caprice over
against dire hunger.

After twenty centuries of Christianity, the world is essentially anti-Christian. The great precept of love calls for justice
and underlines the essential equality between human beings. It
would have us regard all human beings as brothers and sisters

and other Christs and turn the world into a haven of communion. Today it remains an idle word and a vain slogan. The
most serious aspect of the matter is that the very part of the
world that considers itself Christian and has grown up in the
Christian tradition seems to be the most inhuman and ex-
ploitative part of the world.

The official church seems to have lost sight of its prophetic
mission of service and criticism. It leads a grimy existence,
often allied to oppressive power structures. Being a Christian
has been reduced to carrying out a set of superficial, hollow
practices. No longer are they grounded on a dynamic, practical
love that would entail justice, equality, and radical opposition
to every kind of inhumanity. Thus the civilization of idolatry
has arisen in the bosom of Christian civilization. Our faith has
lost its dimension of criticism and liberation. We have turned
religion into a cultural act, into the repetition of empty words
and formulas. The golden calf reigns in the heart of Christen-
dom.

Both in the affluent and the impoverished world, human
beings seem to be a means, an object. Official Christianity
languishes, permitting and practicing a way of life that radically contradicts its principles.[1] It never gathers its forces to
raise a clear and determined protest. It is not just that Christians do not display any distinctive character in their dealings
with their non-Christian brothers and sisters. Worse still,
Christians exploit Christians; Christians show no concern
when faced with the hunger of other Christians; Christians
with Cadillacs receive the same fraternal communion as hungry, barefooted Christians do; some Christians go to the moon
and read the Bible in outer space while masses of Christians
cannot even read a newspaper and do not have enough money
to buy a small transistor radio. Being a Christian has been
reduced to a matter of appearances. It is something easy that
one must do in order to be sure of heaven. It is merely a social
practice, not a basic attitude of life oriented toward others. No
one sees official Christianity as a liberative force, as an ally in
the cause of protest—neither the hungry Indians, the lowly
members of the proletariat, the alienated and lonely bureau-

crats, nor the dedicated revolutionaries who have devoted their lives to the cause of a better world.

In the midst of this idolatrous and dehumanized civilization, humanistic atheism presents itself as the liberator of humanity and the champion of authentic humanism. As we have seen in this book, it tends to emphasize faith in human beings rather than denial of God. This faith proposes to be a liberating praxis. As Camus once wrote: "If the world has been, and still is, inhuman with God, then we shall try to humanize it without God or against him." Humanistic atheism rejects all deities who are antagonistic to humanity, all images of a being who prevents us from being fully human.

In that sense modern atheism can clearly help to revitalize and purify authentic Christianity a great deal. It is paving the way for an encounter with the true and authentic God, the God who liberates us. If the struggle for justice (understood in the broadest and fullest sense) seems to be the only way to live humanly today, and if the essence of true religion is to seek justice in practice, then perhaps we should go along with Martin Marty and call atheistic humanism "an ally of faith." From that point of view we can also understand what Tillich meant when he compared the atheist to the mystic, saying that they both have a mission to liberate us from idolatry and lead us to the heart of authentic religion. There is no doubt that humanistic atheism has helped greatly to salvage authentic faith, and that it is still doing so. In all the strands of atheism presented in this book we have been able to glimpse fundamental errors in the way Christians understand and live out their faith. Perhaps now we can appreciate how much truth there is in Ernst Bloch's statement that "only an atheist can be a good Christian, and only a Christian can be a good atheist." Only a faith devoid of idolatries and free to serve people can be a fully Christian faith. Only human beings who are atheists with respect to the gods of consumption and the gods they have made of themselves can recognize the liberating God.

The responsibility of us believers today is vast and heavy. Vatican II itself acknowledged that the scandal of present Christian practice was one of the main causes of present-day atheism. Christians do not display sincere faith and love dedicated to the welfare of their neighbors.

It is not enough to recognize and admit our faults, however. We must radically change our attitude. More than ever before the mission of Christians must be to teach the idolatrous world through their works and their way of life. We must show that a sincere, committed faith is not an excuse for nonaction and alienation; that instead it is a source of dynamic activity and of dedicated commitment to the cause of human liberation. Faith can never serve as an excuse for maintaining injustice and oppression or for evading our task on earth. A faith that turns its back on other people in order to reach God is essentially antireligious and anti-Christian. The only way to get to God is through the concrete faces of our fellow human beings. To leap above real humanity in order to dialogue with God is to find oneself in a narcissistic dialogue with one's own ego. God cannot be an impediment to authentic humanism. God can only be its supreme realization.

Neither atheism nor faith is worth anything if it remains mere ideology. Each must be something more than sterile talk and an intellectual exercise. God is with those committed to justice, not with those who merely sing or talk about it. Atheists and Christians are on the side of authentic religion and God if they are committed to the cause of justice and love in the world. They are against religion and God if they help to maintain injustice and lack of love.

The essence of religion is justice, and God himself is *love*. Atheism can be either oppressive or liberative. Authentic Christianity is essentially *liberation*.

Notes

1. In one of his books Erich Fromm wonders how it is possible for ministers, priests, and rabbis not to raise their most vehement cries of protest against this kind of capitalist society. In Fromm's eyes such a society is totally incompatible with any kind of monotheism. There are exceptions, to be sure, he notes. But on the whole "all churches belong essentially to the conservative forces in modern society and use religion to keep man going and satisfied with a profoundly irreligious system" (*The Sane Society* [New York: Rinehart & Company, 1955], p. 177).

PERSONAL EPILOGUE

My readers, if there are any readers, will probably find this book hasty, unequal, and poorly worked out. I must confess that while I was writing it, I felt an enormous desire to leave it in mid-course. I felt that these were just words, more words, when the only worthwhile thing is committed personal action with the people. I finished the book hurriedly, overcoming myself continually, thinking that perhaps it might help someone after all. I feel no desire at all to go back over it and touch it up. Furthermore, I want these lines to be my final goodbye to the intellectual world. I have felt its attractions, but I think I have discovered its phoniness. Every idea is hollow if it is not fleshed out in real life. I don't really know whether the book I have written is of any value. But as for myself, I am going to try to live out its contents with the oppressed.

OTHER ORBIS TITLES

THE COMING OF THE THIRD CHURCH
An Analysis of the Present and Future of the Church

Walbert Buhlmann

"Not a systematic treatment of contemporary ecclesiology but a popular narrative analogous to Alvin Toffler's Future Shock." America

ISBN 0-88344-069-5 CIP   *Cloth $12.95*
ISBN 0-88344-070-9   *Paper $6.95*

FREEDOM MADE FLESH

Ignacio Ellacuría

"Ellacuría's main thesis is that God's saving message and revelation are historical, that is, that the proclamation of the gospel message must possess the same historical character that revelation and salvation history do and that, for this reason, it must be carried out in history and in a historical way." Cross and Crown

ISBN 0-88344-140-3   *Cloth $8.95*
ISBN 0-88344-141-1   *Paper $4.95*

CHRISTIAN POLITICAL THEOLOGY
A MARXIAN GUIDE

Joseph Petulla

"Petulla presents a fresh look at Marxian thought for the benefit of Catholic theologians in the light of the interest in this subject which was spurred by Vatican II, which saw the need for new relationships with men of all political positions." Journal of Economic Literature

ISBN 0-88344-060-1   *Paper $4.95*

THE NEW CREATION: MARXIST AND CHRISTIAN

José María González Ruiz

"A worthy book for lively discussion." The New Review of Books and Religion
ISBN 0-88344-327-9 CIP   *Cloth $6.95*

CHRISTIANS AND SOCIALISM
Documentation of the Christians for Socialism Movement in Latin America

edited by John Eagleson

"Compelling in its clear presentation of the issue of Christian commitment in a revolutionary world." The Review of Books and Religion
ISBN 0-88344-058-X   *Paper $4.95*

THE CHURCH AND THIRD WORLD REVOLUTION

Pierre Bigo

"Heavily documented, provocative yet reasonable, this is a testament, demanding but impressive." Publishers Weekly
ISBN 0-88344-071-7 CIP   *Cloth $8.95*
ISBN 0-88344-072-5   *Paper $4.95*

THE GOSPEL IN SOLENTINAME

Ernesto Cardenal

"Upon reading this book, I want to do so many things—burn all my other books which at best seem like hay, soggy with mildew. I now know who (not what) is the church and how to celebrate church in the eucharist..The dialogues are intense, profound, radical. The Gospel in Solentiname calls us home." Carroll Stuhlmueller, National Catholic Reporter
ISBN 0-88344-168-3 CIP   *Cloth $6.95*